W9-CTH-285

Axxiety In Relationship

HOW TO OVERCOME
ANXIETY, JEALOUSY,
NEGATIVE THINKING,
MANAGE INSECURITY, AND
ATTACHMENT

LEARN HOW TO ELIMINATE
COUPLES CONFLICTS
TO ESTABLISH BETTER
RELATIONSHIPS

MELANIE WHITE

Copyright - 2022 -

All rights reserved.

The content contained within
this book may not be reproduced,
duplicated or transmitted without
direct written permission from the
author or the publisher.

Under no circumstances will
any blame or legal responsibility
be held against the publisher, or
author, for any damages, reparation,
or monetary loss due to the information
contained within this book. Either directly or
indirectly.

Legal Notice:

This book is copyright protected. This book is only for personal use.
You cannot amend, distribute, sell, use, quote or paraphrase any
part, or the content within this book, without the consent of the
author or publisher.

Disclaimer Notice:

Please note the information contained within this document is for
educational and entertainment purposes only. All effort has been
executed to present accurate, up to date, and reliable, complete
information. No warranties of any kind are declared or implied.
Readers acknowledge that the author is not engaging in the
rendering of legal, financial, medical or professional advice. The
content within this book has been derived from various sources.
Please consult a licensed professional before attempting any
techniques outlined in this book.

By reading this document, the reader agrees that under no
circumstances is the author responsible for any losses, direct or
indirect, which are incurred as a result of the use of information
contained within this document, including, but not limited to, -
errors, omissions, or inaccuracies.

TABLE OF CONTENTS

CHAPTER 6.

CHAPTER 7.

CHAPTER 8.

CHAPTER 9.

CHAPTER 10.

CHAPTER 17.

CHAPTER 18.

CHAPTER 19.

CHAPTER 20.

CHAPTER 21.

INTRODUCTION

A nxiety is part of all life activities; it is also a universal and emotional feeling. Its natural role is to alert us to potential threats so that we can assess and respond to them effectively. This increased readiness can also allow people to increase their efficiency and enhance innovative drives. Anxiety is also seen as a phenomenon in contemporary society and is increasingly reflected in the arts, music, literature, and social media. This condition induces excessive or exaggerated reactions to potential risks, leading to chronic and debilitating symptoms related to disorganization such as fear, phobia, and repetitive behaviors, which also undermine the lives of other people.

Anxiety is a normal human condition and a necessary part of our lives. We all have trait anxiety in one form or another. In "fight or flight mode," fear allows us to recognize and respond to dangers. This will inspire us to face difficult challenges. The "right" level of fear will allow us to do more and inspire innovations and practices. However, anxiety can be seen from another perspective. Persistent anxiety caused by significant emotional issues can lead to discomfort and, in the worst cases, cause disturbances such as obsession. At this point, anxiety can have profoundly distressing and impaired effects on our lives and our physical and mental health.

The feeling of widespread fear is supported by research commissioned by the Mental Health Foundation. Disturbingly, nearly 1 in 5 people have reported active anxiety "almost every day" or "almost all the time." The study indicates that "finances, expenses, and debts" are the most common causes of anxiety and may represent the effect of unemployment and inflation on public health and well-being. Furthermore, half of the population has reported that "people are more depressed than they were five years ago." Anxiety is among the most widely identified, underdiagnosed, and undertreated conditions within the mental health community. A good ability to cope with anxiety is the secret to survival in the face of life. However, knowing it too often means we risk losing our real selves, finding a balance, or relaxing and healing in our lives. We can always do an important action for our well-being if we only seek a little inner harmony.

This study looks at anxiety as a core component of our nature and part of the natural reaction to human emotions. This is also a challenging stigma, which still prevents us from finding support and assistance when our anxiety is becoming a real problem. As individuals and communities, we need to fully understand and participate in anxiety programs, identify the warning signs in ourselves, and make sure we have methods to manage it when it tends to harm our emotions. We need to consider whether others around us, such as friends, family, and colleagues, are experiencing or at risk of distressing anxiety due to life events and circumstances. Community public health initiatives need to identify areas of high anxiety and include a non-stigmatizing and easily accessible continuum of care. To identify the best places and alliances for those 1 in 5 people who have problems most of the time, we urge public health commissioners to look at the list of common sources from an online survey and use them as a benchmark. We believe that public policy will benefit significantly from "fear awareness" and from changing its policies and modes of public interaction to avoid and reduce anxiety. If we honestly understand the rising costs to individuals, their future children, families, and employers of anxiety, then we must act now. This is one of the foundations of this book.

It takes a while to stop worrying and keep our anxious thoughts under tight control. Often these thoughts leave us and we begin to feel overwhelmed. Other people have chronic anxiety, leading to daily unpleasant or even distressing physical symptoms, which can grow and cause life-limiting effects. Fear can also cause these feelings. Going through troubling circumstances can throw us off balance, but overcoming them can have a positive effect on our lives.

Anxiety will work for or against us in an emotional state. It is something that we all share but that varies from person to person depending on how we experience joy and respond to it. Our lives, our upbringing, and our personalities can influence an individual's behavior toward fear during an experience.

Getting depressed is not a sign of weakness, but anyone with these symptoms needs to see a counselor or psychiatrist.

However, once you begin to understand anxiety better, you can do a lot to reduce the pressure and learn to feel the full spectrum of emotions without thinking about them.

CHAPTER - 1
WHAT IS ANXIETY IN PEOPLE?

S ide effects of anxiety typically include unattainable fears and physiological problems, such as an upset stomach or rapid heartbeat. Anxiety is likely to arise from a combination of factors such as genetics, brain structure, attitude, and life events. Even though it can be successfully treated, the goal is not to completely eradicate anxiety but to reduce it to a reasonable level. With proper treatment, many people end up feeling much better instantly or within a couple of weeks.

Unfortunately, anxiety disorder is still common. Research reveals that one in four adults will experience it in their lifetime and that one in ten children is also likely to suffer anxiety issues in their early years. This condition seems to be the most prevalent mental health problem in women and is only surpassed by Methamphetamine use. Anxiety disorders can make it hard to study, work, perform daily tasks, and get along with others. People often suffer this ailment for years before they can be diagnosed and treated. If you suspect that you are feeling anxiety issues, it is best to seek professional treatment as quickly as possible. This illness can be treated, and early diagnosis can help ensure successful treatment.

What Is Normal Anxiety?

Anxiety can also be critical to your survival in certain cases. If you believe that something dangerous is going to happen, the brain will send a message to the rest of the body, and the body will respond through the release of dopamine, which gives us a sense of strength and alertness and prepares us to attack (fight) or flee to survive (flight). Adrenaline surges can also have negative side effects. These may include nervousness, anxiety, dizziness, sweating, tremors, or shortness of breath. These symptoms can be alarming, but they do not last and do not affect the body.

Anxiety is part of our experience and also an integral component of humanity. In addition, it is also a psychological condition that we have in common with animals when we are faced with a threat to our well-being or our survival. Fear is a common emotion that increases anticipation, desires, and neurological function in the body and activates other behavioral tendencies that allow us to cope with danger. However, how do we differentiate between anxiety and fear, since both are also used as synonyms? Although fear often has an immediate response causing classic fight or flight reflexes, an unconscious fear reaction is faster than conscious thought and spikes of adrenaline are released, which can subside until the expected or actual danger passes. This can be an ambiguous and uncomfortable feeling in anticipation of other misfortunes that are not clearly described.

The committee that revised the diagnostic criteria for the most recent version of the DSM2 also distinguishes anxiety from fears as a "warning response to real or extreme (real or perceived) danger" as "a potential mood in final planning of possible negative events." In this sense, the symptoms of fear versus anxiety can diverge and converge to different degrees. The way people perceive various forms of anxiety and how they present themselves to the public at different points on the spectrum. Discusses everyday events and what arises when anxiety is more than a floating phenomenon and is perceived as a set of shortcomings or a permanent presence in one's life. Anxiety disorders such as fear, phobias, repetitive behavior, excessive distaste for certain objects, exposure to certain physical settings or places, or a constant worry that something unpleasant will happen in the future can trigger painful memories. A defining feature of anxiety is the persistence and interruption of depressive symptoms, including irritability and concentration. Most people have physical disorders, such as palpitations, swelling, pain, rapid and heavy breathing, dizziness, fainting, indigestion, upset stomach, nausea, and diarrhea. Some circumstances can completely dominate the life of the worst types of anxiety and the struggle to relax or achieve normal sleep patterns, unfortunately, getting caught up in repetitive patterns of thinking can hinder the ability to maintain desired lifestyles.

How Does Anxiety Affect Us?

Every time danger triggers the flight reflex, it affects all three "work systems:" your thinking (cognitive), feeling and function of your body (physical), and your actions (behavioral).

These three structures change according to personality and situation:

1. **Cognitive:** The emphasis shifts immediately and unconsciously to the potential danger. The influence on a person's mindset can range from mild to high.
2. **Physical:** Panic attacks or increased heart rate, rapid breathing, sweating, nausea or dizziness, feeling "weak in the knees," tremors, tense muscles, shortness of breath,

and vomiting are common symptoms.

3. **Behavior:** People act in certain ways to protect themselves from anxiety (e.g., taking self-defense lessons or avoiding dark streets). It is important to understand that anxiety mechanisms in cognitive, physical, and physiological responses frequently move together. You probably feel physically unwell and nervous and spend a lot of time analyzing your family budget and spending (behavior) if, for example, you spend too much time worrying about your finances (cognitive). Or you may worry about doing your best (cognitive), feel anxious, and maybe even get "butterflies" (physical) when you put off studying and then plan to do it at the last minute (behavioral).

The points to consider about anxiety are the following:

- It is natural for any living being.
- It is critical for life and adaptation.
- It is not harmful.
- It is usually short-lived.
- It is often positive for tests (at low or intermediate levels).

When Is Anxiety a Problem?

Everyone has signs of anxiety, but they usually don't cause problems. However, if the cognitive, physical, and behavioral symptoms of anxiety are persistent and severe, and the anxiety in a person's life is distressing to the point of negatively affecting the person's ability to work or learn, socialize, and perform activities daily, you can go beyond healthy limits.

Examples of anxiety disorder can be seen in:

1. **Cognitive:** Worrying thoughts (e.g., "I lose control");

worrying expectations (e.g., "I'm about to slur my words and feel embarrassed"); worrying beliefs (e.g., "only the poor care").

2. **Physical:** Irregular underlying physical symptoms (e.g., heartbeat and dyspnea in response to center). Symptoms of clinical anxiety can be mistaken for real signs of illness, including a heart attack.

3. **Behavior:** Avoidance of unpleasant conditions (e.g., driving), avoidance of activities that generate emotions similar to those experienced when under stress (e.g., exercise), subtle prevention (behavioral actions designed to distract a person, e.g., talking to others in times of anxiety), and constructive behavior (e.g., habits to reduce anxiety and feel "safer"). Several factors determine whether or not these behaviors are anxious.

Anxiety Disorders

The period or extent of a feeling of distress may, in some cases, be disproportionate to the original trigger or stressor. Physical signs and symptoms, such as high blood pressure and nausea, may also develop. These responses go beyond stress and anxiety. The APA defines a person with an anxiety disorder as "having persistent intrusive thoughts or problems." As soon as stress and anxiety reach the stage of an illness, they can make daily function difficult.

It's typical to feel anxious about transferring to a new area, starting a new job, or taking a test. This type of anxiety is unpleasant but it can inspire you to work harder and do a much better job. Ordinary anxiety is a feeling that repeats itself; however, it does not interfere with your daily life. When it comes to an anxiety condition, the feeling of fear can be with you at all times. It is intense and also often paralyzing.

This type of anxiety can cause you to stop doing things you like. In extreme cases, it can prevent you from getting into an elevator, crossing the street, or even leaving your house. If left unattended, the anxiety will undoubtedly continue to worsen. Anxiety problems are one of the most common types of mental illness and can affect anyone at any age. According to the American Psychiatric Organization, women are more likely than men to be identified as having an anxiety problem.

CHAPTER -2
WHAT IS RELATIONSHIP ANXIETY?

G ood relationships can be one of the most interesting and enjoyable things in life. It is something most of us look forward to experiencing and building on. However, thinking about the complexities involved in a relationship can be a fertile breeding ground for feelings and thoughts that lead to anxiety. Anxiety in a relationship can arise at any stage of dating or even marriage. Many young people may have feelings of anxiety and stress just thinking about being in a relationship. In the early stages of a relationship, people may have feelings of insecurity that lead to more anxiety. One may experience troubling thoughts such as "Does this person like me?" "How serious is this, relationship?" "Will it work?"

One might think that feelings of anxiety in the early stages of a relationship will subside once the person realizes that the relationship will last, for example by getting married or even knowing that the partner will not hurt them. Well, this is not always the case. For some couples, feelings of anxiety become more intense as the two people get closer. Destabilizing thoughts come flooding like a storm: "Do I like this person?" "Do I want to spend the rest of my life with him/her?" "Will he/she lose interest in me?" "Am I good enough?".

All of these concerns can make a person feel lonely even when in a relationship. These anxiety-triggering thoughts can cause a person to distance themselves from their partner. Worse, relationship anxiety can cause us to give up on love altogether. Therefore, it is important to understand anxiety and its triggers and consequences. Knowing about relationship anxiety can help us spot the negative thoughts and actions that sabotage our love lives. How can you control anxious feelings and overcome relationship-destroying feelings?

Honestly speaking, falling in love and being in love challenges us in numerous ways. Many of these challenges are unexpected, and when we first face them, our human nature puts us on the defensive. For example, if you love someone very much and they break your heart, you will most likely avoid being vulnerable. At some level, we all fear being hurt, knowingly or unknowingly. Ironically, this fear tends to increase when we get what we want. If a relationship is good, we begin to fear the "shock of a breakup." Consequently, we begin to take up the defense, creating distance and eventually ending the relationship. If we are experiencing love and being treated in an unusually good way, we become tense.

That defensive tension becomes a barrier. It's important to keep in mind that anxiety in a relationship doesn't arise just because of situations that happen between the two parties involved. This feeling can also arise due to our perception. The things you tell yourself about a relationship, love, attraction, desire, etc., will affect your life. This means that you may have the best partner in the world, but still, your thoughts prevent you from noticing and enjoying the moment. The proverbial "inner voice" is very dangerous if it is negative. This mental couch can tell us things that fuel our fear of intimacy. The critical inner voice can give us bad advice like: "You are too ugly for him/her," "Even other people have left you before," and "You cannot trust such a man/woman." What do such thoughts do? They make us turn against the people we love and, more importantly, against ourselves. The critical inner voice can make us hostile, paranoid, and unnecessarily suspicious. It can also push our feelings of defense, mistrust, anxiety, and jealousy to unhealthy levels. This little negative voice feeds us an endless stream of unhealthy thoughts that worry us about relationships and undermine our happiness. It prevents us from enjoying life healthily.

The main challenge arises once we focus on these thoughts. We get in our heads and focus on whatever that minute of thought is saying. Then we process it, reflect on it, grill it, and grill it again until it looks like an immovable mountain. At that moment, we are distracted from our partner, so there is no real relationship or interaction. After elaborating on the thoughts, we can begin to act, either immaturely or destructively. For example, one might start bossing the partner around, watching their every move, making unnecessary nasty comments, ignoring or mistreating the other.

Let's say your partner is staying late at work or stopping by the local bar for a drink before you get home. Critical inner-thinking will trigger thoughts like "Where is he/she? What is he/she doing?" "With whom and why? Does he/she prefer to be away from home? Maybe he/she doesn't love me anymore." These thoughts can go through your mind so much that when your partner comes home, you feel completely insecure, paranoid, angry, and defensive. In this state, it becomes difficult to have a constructive conversation about their whereabouts. Consequently, this partner will feel misunderstood and frustrated. In addition, he will also adopt a defensive posture. Soon, the dynamic of the relationship changes from pleasure and comfort to irrational and unfair treatment. Instead of enjoying the rest of the night, it is wasted because everyone feels withdrawn and upset.

Do you realize that, in such a case, you have effectively created the distance you initially feared? Or do you also realize that your partner might not have had negative intentions? The fact is that the distance you have created was not caused by the situation itself or the circumstances, no. It was triggered by that critical inner voice that might have been wrong. That voice colored your thinking with negativity, distorted your perception, and ultimately led to self-destruction.

The biggest challenge that leads to self-destruction in relationships is self-doubt. If we evaluate most of the situations that concern us in a relationship, we realize that we can handle the consequences. Most of us are resilient enough to experience heartbreak and heal. It's probably happened before, and you didn't die from it. However, our inner voice tends to exaggerate things, especially negative ones. That voice terrifies and catastrophizes everything, making it hard to stay rational. It can trigger serious bouts of anxiety over some nonexistent relationship dynamics that don't even exist and strange, intangible threats.

Breakups probably wouldn't be as painful if we didn't have that critical voice. It is what analyzes everything and destroys us by pointing out all our flaws and the things we fail to do. The distorted reality makes us think that we are neither strong nor resistant enough to survive. That critical voice is the negative friend who is always giving bad advice: "You can't survive heartbreak, just stay on your guard and don't make yourself vulnerable."

We form our defenses depending on life's unique experiences and adaptations. The inner voice also borrows from those unique experiences. If a partner says that he would leave you because you are overweight or underweight, the inner voice will use that line to distort reality. It will make you think that another colleague is noticing the same flaws and will go for them. When we feel insecure or anxious, some of us tend to despair or cling to our actions. Others become control freaks, wanting to possess the partner. A large number of people begin to feel crowded, as if there is no respite in the relationship, thus choosing to distance themselves from their loved ones.

In extreme cases, we let go of feelings of desire in our relationship. We can start to be aloof, cautious, or completely withdrawn. Such patterns of attachment and relationship may stem from our early life experiences. In the childhood years, we unconsciously develop attachment patterns depending on our environment.

Patterns become the blueprint for our adult lives. They influence how we assess our needs and how we satisfy them. These attachment patterns and styles are the main determinants of the amount of anxiety we feel in a relationship.

CHAPTER - 3

WHAT IS ANXIETY IN PEOPLE?

When you start a relationship, the initial stage can make you worried and tense with different questions in your head, asking for answers. You start thinking, "Does he like me?" "Will this work?" "How serious is this going to get?"

It's sad to know that these worries don't subside in the later stages of the relationship when you're plagued with anxiety. The closer and more intimate you become in a relationship, the greater the intensity of anxiety can be.

Worry, stress, and anxiety about your relationships can leave you feeling lonely and despondent. You can unknowingly create a distance between yourself and your loved one. Another serious consequence of anxiety is its ability to make us give up love altogether. That's pretty devastating because love is a very beautiful thing. It's important to understand what makes you so anxious in a relationship and why you feel so insecure and attached. I will explain some of the reasons in the following paragraphs.

Falling in love demands of you in countless ways, more ways than you can imagine. The more you appreciate a person, the more you can lose. How ironic is that? This intense feeling of love and the powerful emotions that accompany it, consciously and unconsciously, create in you the fear of being hurt and the fear of the unknown.

Oddly enough, this fear comes as a result of being treated exactly how you want to be treated in your relationship. When you begin to experience love, as it should be, or when you are treated tenderly and affectionately, something unfamiliar to you, you may be overcome with anxiety.

Most of the time, it's not just the events that happen between you and your partner that lead to anxiety. It's the things you say to yourself and feed your mind about those events that ultimately lead to anxiety. Your biggest critic, who is also the "bad coach" in your head, can criticize you and feed you bad advice that will ultimately fuel your fear of intimacy. It is this petty critic who suggests that:

- "You are not smart, he/she would soon get bored of you."
- "You will never meet anyone who loves you, so why try?"
- "Don't trust him, he's probably looking for a better person."
- "She/he doesn't love you. Get out before you get hurt."

This means that the coach in your head manipulates you and turns you against yourself and the people you love. He fosters hostility and you soon discover that you are paranoid. You become suspicious of every move your partner makes; this lowers your self-esteem and leads to unhealthy levels of mistrust, defensiveness, jealousy, anxiety, and stress.

What this means is that you are training your head to constantly feed yourself with thoughts that jeopardize your happiness and make you worry about your relationship instead of simply allowing yourself to enjoy it. When you start to focus so much on these unhealthy thoughts, you distract yourself from the real relationship, which involves healthy communication and love with your partner.

You soon discover that you are reacting to unnecessary issues and making nasty and destructive comments. She/he can also become childish or fatherly with their partner.

For example, your partner comes home from work and doesn't have a good appetite, so they politely decline dinner. Sitting alone after a while, your inner critic freaks out and asks, "How can you refuse my food? What have you eaten all day? Who has been bringing you food at work? Can I believe you?" These thoughts can continually grow in your mind until you feel insecure, angry, and moody the next morning. You may start to act cold or angry, and this can put your partner off, frustrate them, and put them on the defensive. They won't know what's been going on in your head, so it will seem like your behavior comes out of nowhere.

In just a few short hours, you have successfully changed the dynamic of your relationship. Instead of savoring the time you spend together, you can spend an entire day feeling worried and apart from each other. What you have just done is to initiate and enthrone the distance that you feared so much. The factor responsible for this turn of events is not the situation itself, it is that critical inner voice that clouded your thoughts, distorted your perceptions, suggested bad opinions, and led you down a disastrous path as a result.

When it comes to the problems you worry about a lot in your relationship, what you don't know—and what your inner critic doesn't tell you, is that you are stronger and more resilient than you think. The reality is that you can handle the hurts, rejections, and disappointments that you fear so much. We are made in such a way that it is possible to absorb negative situations, heal from them and deal with them. You can experience pain and ultimately heal and come out stronger. However, the bad coach in your head, that critical inner voice, in most cases puts you under pressure and makes reality seem like a tragedy. He/she creates scenarios in your head that don't exist and brings to light threats that aren't tangible. Even when, in reality, there are real problems and unhealthy situations, that inner voice in your head will magnify such situations and tear you apart in ways you don't deserve. It will completely misrepresent the reality of the situation and cloud your resilience and determination. It will always give you unpleasant opinions and advice.

However, these critical voices you hear in your head are formed as a result of your unique experiences and what you have adapted to over time. When you feel anxious or insecure, there is a tendency to become overly attached and desperate in your actions. Possession and control over your partner are established. On the other hand, you may feel an intrusion into your relationship. You may begin to withdraw from your partner and separate yourself from your emotional desires. He may start to act uncommunicative or withdraw.

These problem response patterns may stem from their early attachment styles. These style patterns influence how you react to your needs and how you go about meeting them.

Signs of Insecure Attachment

Some practices are triggered by attachments as a result of insecurity. A variety of undesirable practices can appear in early adolescence due to unreliable connections.

Too Demanding

For example, you don't want your partner to do things without you. You desire to burn most of their extra time together. You solicit their time and consideration to the detriment of other friendships and relationships.

Doubt or Jealousy

For example, you are suspicious of the behavior of your partner or colleague and of the general population with whom you work. You question their work connections and who they communicate with within the work environment.

You are suspicious of anyone you feel is getting too close, as you fear they will leave you for someone else.

Lack of Emotional Intimacy

For example, your partner feels that he or she cannot honestly get close to you. They portray you as someone who "sets dividers" or say that you are normally difficult to approach internally.

Enthusiastic Dependency

You rely on your companion or partner for your enthusiastic prosperity. You desire that your joy originates from your relationship.

If you are upset, it is because you believe that your partner or companion does not satisfy you.

Frightening

You want closeness in your connections. However, your experience has been that if you get too close to your loved one, they will hurt you. This makes you have mixed feelings.

You draw your partner closer and then pull them away when it becomes "too much." Your fear of getting too close, as you would rather not be hurt, makes your relationship suffer.

Lack of Trust

You don't trust your partner for fear that they will undermine you or abandon you. You're afraid of telling them something or revealing a part of you that they won't like and that will push them to end the relationship.

Anger Issues

Getting unnecessarily angry is also a sign of insecure attachment in a relationship. When you start a fight over a problem that could be resolved amicably, it shows that you are not ready to tolerate your partner or that you are fed up with their excesses. This behavior, if not addressed, can negatively affect the relationship. Let me conclude by saying that when you express your insecurities, you begin to drive your partner away from you, thus creating a self-fulfilling prophecy. By self-fulfilling prophecy, I mean validating and bringing to life those negative thoughts that come into your mind, also known as your inner voice. It's starting to look like that voice was right after all. But no, it wasn't right. The fight is internal and continues regardless of the circumstances. When you live with anxiety, your life might be like a fairy tale, but that inner voice will still have something negative to point out. It's important to deal with your insecurities without dragging your partner into them. You can do it by following two steps:

1. Uncover the roots of your insecurities and find out what led to them.
2. Challenge the critical inner voice and petty coach that obstructs the free flow of love in your relationship.

CHAPTER - 4

RELATIONSHIP STABILITY AND WHY PEOPLE LOOK FOR IT

The best thing you can do in those situations is to commit to your partner consistently. How do you get along with your partner? What is your form of communication? You can talk about problems repeatedly, but it's hard to fix unresolved issues if you don't lower yourself to your partner's level by communicating. The good news is that you will work with your partner to overcome romantic vulnerability. It requires time, efficient communication, and the ability to strengthen your relationship.

Here's how to deal with emotional insecurities:

Meet the Needs of Others

- Every person in the world has several basic needs;
- We are all committed to making sure we can escape pain and suffering;
- We want diversity in life;
- We want to feel important;

Therefore, connecting with others is crucial.

All needs are in the hierarchy of how important they are. You need to know your spouse's most important need.

Does your relationship help meet your emotional needs? If not, how can you change the way your partner is treated and appreciated?

Balance Polarity

In any normal relationship, there is always masculine and feminine energy. Such energy sources must not be related to gender, but opposite powers must be present to achieve romantic peace.

This definition is known as polarity. Have you built a unique relationship with your partner? It can cause anxiety when both partners take on masculine or feminine traits. These positions have changed over time. How can polarity be restored and insecurity outlawed in a relationship?

Take Care of Yourself as a New Couple

New couples want to get to know each other and actively get closer whenever they can. This initial desire disappears over time. Once you get to know your partner better, you both seem to not treasure and adore each other as much. The routine of daily life causes you to relax and stop pleasing your spouse.

Insecurities will begin to show when your partner feels that your attraction to them has faded. During this time, it is important to restore your love and behave as you did when you first started dating. Love your spouse more than your friends. Appreciate your spouse by complimenting and scheduling amazing dates. Be considerate and write them love notes. This small behavior can lead to lower anxiety and make your partner feel desired.

Create New Memories

Mistakes are bound to happen in any relationship, but both of you need to make sure they don't stick around. Also, if you've fought over financial matters before, it's time to put those old issues behind you if you want to move forward as a couple.

Try to change your attitude instead of demanding that your partner stop doing what worries you. Be supportive of your partner and decide together to create a new and delightful story instead of easing the pain of the past.

Occasional insecurity exists in the most stable relationships. You can't control your partner's feelings, but you should do everything you can to support them.

What Do You Do if This Kills Your Vulnerability?

Jealousy is cute at first, but it can lead to a poisonous wedge between partners. Many of us experience doubts, which is natural, from time to time. However, it can drive a wedge between you and your partner when it leads to personal insecurity and discussion of differences.

In some ways, vulnerability is good because it makes your relationship more intimate and increases the value of your partner. But, if there is too much fear, it will create a toxic environment and damage your confidence. Insecurity can also separate couples who love and care for each other.

When doubt or jealousy first comes to light, the partner always seems innocent and a little cute. However, it can cause you to act out of control in a relationship that seems to be going well. To improve your relationship, you and your partner must make resolutions. Here are some examples that both of you should focus on.

1. **Self-esteem:** It is difficult to remove, but in it lies your negative mentality, which makes it difficult to eliminate.

Improving your self-esteem is the best way to get rid of (or at least decrease) your insecurities. How can you do that? Get excited by booking a relaxing day at the spa, starting to work out, or doing something you want. It's best to focus on a problem you want to get rid of and build on it.

2. **Find the root cause:** You cannot rule out any obstacles until you accept that they exist. Dig deep and think about your existing relationship to find out what is causing you so much pain. Was there something your mother said that stuck with you from the age of five? Is your partner doing something that challenges your motivation?

   Either way, if you know the source of your fear, then you're ready to face it.

3. **Trust yourself and your partner:** No one will be surprised to admit that trust is the main factor for a happy and healthy relationship. The term "trust" just means sharing your deepest secrets with your spouse.

   You also need to have faith in your instincts. If you've never had a reason to distrust your spouse, don't! However, if you feel that something is not quite right in your mind, trust your instincts!

4. **Stop overthinking:** Don't think of it as a personal problem when your partner decides they want to hang out with their friends one night without you. Not everything your partner does is supposed to hurt you. If your partner falls asleep earlier, it doesn't mean he's cheating on you, it just means he's tired.

5. **You both need room to breathe and have a healthy relationship:** It will help prevent your partner from feeling smothered or attacked. You must also follow your interests and strive to preserve your own social life. Doing things

for yourself will improve your confidence. Keep in mind that beyond your romantic relationships you still have your own life to live.

6. **Leave the negative past:** Previous encounters will ruin your love life. You should stop looking back at how a mysterious ex made you feel before he brought insecurities into your new relationship. Only if you let go of your bad memories will you be able to move on.

   Talk to a therapist, friend, family, or your current spouse about your past encounters; "sometimes it's cathartic to let it all go." Talking honestly about past painful experiences will help your new partner understand you better. And, let's face it, it's just cathartic to let it go sometimes.

7. **Don't stop talking:** Talking is an important aspect of interaction and in relationships, it's some of the most common dating advice you'll see often.

8. **Be careful about your time on social media:** Many distractions are rampant on social media today. Some women flaunt their nudity on all social networks, and this can make you compare their body shape with the shape of your spouse, making you feel that your partner's shape is horrible. Everyone on social media only posts the best photos and the best moments.

   Not to mention, if you're inclined to harass your partner's exes on social media, it won't help you get over your insecurities.

9. **Discuss with real friends how you feel:** Nobody wants to be alone, why should you talk to a group of good friends about your feelings? If you have an amazing group of friends, gather the most trusted ones and share your innermost feelings and thoughts.

Discussing your problems not only alleviates some of the fears you have, but also your friends can share their personal experiences to resolve issues of confusion or envy.

10. **Channel your anxieties into something positive:** If you want to rule out petty jealousy in relationships, start exercising or do something constructive whenever possible. This may sound crazy, but it will motivate you to improve your self-esteem and promote good mental health for at least 30 minutes a day.

    Research indicates that daily exercise can help lower anxiety and depression and, at the same time, promotes a good mood.

How Obsessive Attachment Impacts Couples

The theory of evolution, in addition to its conceptual and empirical implications, is a valuable and important tool for understanding the nature of personalities, relationships, and impact controls. Several research studies on the origins and associations of individual variations in adult attachment patterns have been conducted in the past two decades. However, a major drawback of previous studies is that many do not take into account the effect of contexts on dependency speech. This is surprising because evolutionary theory is essentially a "person by circumstance" interactionist framework, probably stemming from the lack of methods that would allow such a dynamic approach.

Although substantial insights have also been gained from historical studies of attachment expression, there is currently little information on how attachment types are expressed at the moment and how they are articulated in a real-life context.

Evolutionary theory is a philosophy that suggests that people are born with an inherent motivational mechanism (called a behavioral attachment mechanism), which is activated in times of real or symbolic danger, causing the person to seek proximity to relieve anxiety and win a relationship in the sense of protection. The key to the theory is, based on his accumulated history of experiences with attached personalities, that the individual constructs affective-behavioral representations or "personal working models." These models help to analyze and play an important role in controlling the knowledge of the social environment throughout its life cycle.

Most of the work on attachment in adults focuses on forms and assessment of attachment. In general, attachment style can be conceptualized in terms of security and vulnerability. Repeated experiences with emotionally accessible and sensitive attachment figures facilitate the construction of a healthy personality type, with optimistic internal models and constructive techniques for coping with anxiety. Rather, the risks of forming unhealthy attachment types that characterize any use of the negative inner self and/or other constructs and the use of less appropriate regulatory approaches are repeated encounters with contradictory and unresponsive figures.

While there are a plethora of definitions and measures of vulnerability in relationships, it is typically characterized in intimate relationships by high levels of worry and/or avoidance. Fear of relationships reflects a desire for closeness and concern about being excluded or cut off from meaningful relationships, while avoidance of attachments indicates deep self-sufficiency and discomfort with others. Both types of schemes include different secondary acquisition strategies for pain management. People with attachment depression prefer to use the hyperarousal (or optimization) approach. Additionally, previous empirical research has shown that relationship anxiety has been associated with greater negative emotional reactions, greater identification of environmental threats, and negative psychological views.

Individuals with stable attachment only showed more positive effects than those with vulnerability. Furthermore, while variation in the emotional state did not differ between groups, participants with a secure style endured more severe positive mental states in all social settings, and participants with an insecure style endured more severe negative emotional experiences, particularly when they were alone. The results of investigations supported the idea that attachment types have a large impact on cognitive experiences, but the significant limitations of this analysis were that only observations comparing stable and vulnerable participants were published. Therefore, further analytical work is required to investigate how stylistic relationship expressions are articulated in everyday life and how the interaction of attachment types with the environment produces specific experiential tendencies at the moment. Illustrating the importance of reactive attachment disorder in interactions with real-world encounters potentially informed by an individual's personality type would illustrate the relevance of the form of attachment style in the particular sense in which the individual is attached. Therefore, the recognition of changes in attachment style in the sense of social activities can improve our understanding of how the types of relationships function in the social environment.

marital satisfaction & the life cycle

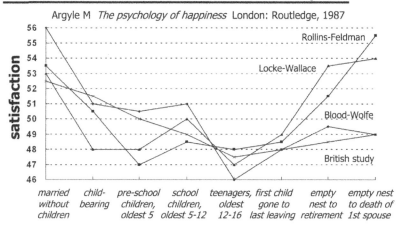

Argyle M *The psychology of happiness* London: Routledge, 1987

Researchers have known mature love for more than three centuries as one of the fundamental psychological needs and its absence contributes to psychological deficits. The components of mature love are:

- Desire
- Passion
- Fellowship
- Honesty

Romantic relationships create an atmosphere for growth that ultimately motivates people to know more and make money. Everyone's self-awareness, confidence, and mental well-being improve during this state, making for a more established relationship. Instead, teenage love seems to build a social atmosphere that is evolutionarily adaptive. Intangible love is made up of:

- Strength
- Possession
- Security
- Grace
- Immorality

Such traits manifest in teenage love as obsessive thoughts. The person whose love trait can be called obsessive love is an individual who finds it difficult to trust their partner and continually tests them. This trait will surely have negative consequences. Many psychologists claim that an addictive model of love is close to substance abuse. Obsessive love as a drug has detrimental implications for life, society, and the family. To achieve the desired emotional impact, a significantly higher attitude is needed. If you try to avoid taking action (e.g., feeling helpless or lonely if you are not in a relationship, feeling sad and permanent, as if you stopped drinking alcohol), there is a subjective desire to stay the course of your behaviors. There is a persistent inability or failure to decrease or regulate the behavior for a longer period than expected.

Obsessive love can affect the dynamics and cultural effects of social learning. Developmental events, such as the growth of children's social bonds, can create an obsessive effect. According to research, people are born into a state of attachment called a psychobiological pattern. Through this program, a baby can stay close to adults and improve their chances of survival; The purpose of this program is to achieve health, confidence, and security in children.

There are three styles of attachments:

- Free
- Avoidable
- Apathetic

These three types are important to be attentive to the needs of children in the early years of a child. Due to the one-antenna theory, an attachment network is not restricted to childhood and involves interpersonal interactions (e.g., families, romantic relationships, etc.).

You evaluate yourself as beautiful and important.

Ambivalent individuals have dysfunctional behaviors and feelings. They are very dependent on others; they fear being left behind and falling in love with others. Deceptive individuals and less complex relationships were recorded in avoiding subjects.

Both romantic partners often disagree. Although it is likely to find disagreements, those who are extremely satisfied with the relationship vary widely among themselves. Conflict management is associated with greater happiness in relationships and greater social well-being. Greater tension in relationships and lower well-being are also correlated with a lack of dialogue.

Since conflict involves important aspects of family interaction, it is essential to investigate how these particular conflict techniques are produced. Annexation theory offers a consistent framework for explaining how different types of conflict occur in the context of intimate relationships. Although researchers have recorded clear connections between attachment types and conflict behaviors, further elucidation of the mechanisms that link these two structures remains an important area of study to establish explanatory procedures that can become the object of therapeutic intervention.

CHAPTER - 5

RELATIONSHIP
INSECURITY

I seemed to destroy every romantic relationship I had been involved in; neither for infidelity nor for incompatibility; not even because of fights, boredom, or the need for personal space. They were all destroyed due to a trance state that regularly consumed my entire being, almost as if I were possessed by a demonic entity. I'd become hypervigilant, as observant as a private investigator. I would become a quick and intensely sharp manipulator. Warm anxiety-infused energy swelled rapidly from my feet to my stomach, all the way to my throat. I would lose control of my thoughts and words. All of these symptoms were caused by my obsession with my partner's past. I would bombard my partner with personal questions about their past relationships. No stone would be left unturned and the obsessions would fester for days, weeks, months, and years at a time. A glance of imaginary visions and thoughts of my partner's past passed through my mind minute after minute without respite. When I finally went to sleep, I would suffer a flood of nightmares, watching these reimagined past encounters with my partner unfold like a movie.

Upon awakening, I would name, blame, and call my partner all sorts of derogatory names. I wasn't aware enough to control the outside assault on the world and the people around me.

As a result, I lost wonderful people in my life. I felt sick as if I had some kind of virus in my bloodstream.

It wasn't until I was in a serious relationship in my mid-twenties that I realized this behavior wasn't the norm and didn't meet my standards and values of what was wrong or right. Up until this point, I couldn't imagine how someone couldn't agree with me and be okay with their partner having some sort of intimate past with someone else. After a particularly vicious fight caused by RJ (Retroactive Jealousy) with my partner, I saw him get so angry and break down that it forced me to see clearly for the first time that my behavior was fueled by jealousy and not sound thinking. After this epiphany, I realized that I didn't want to lose another close person in my life, and deep down, I knew it was time for a change.

I met Sarah four years before we started our relationship. Meeting at a mutual friend's house, we quickly became friends. Because the friendship lasted for many years before the relationship began, I learned much of her history and encounters based on intimate relationships. This information would be used as ammunition in my future jealousy-fueled assaults. As the relationship progressed and we became a couple, I would ask her more and more about her past, filling in mental timelines and imaginary puzzle pieces to create my personalized images of what I thought happened, with cunningly gathered bits of information and not so clever.

At the beginning of the relationship, she would easily and innocently give in to my requests for information.

My newly gathered information would trigger a fit of emotional insecurity in me, and she would be left confused and distraught. She was a quick learner and realized that when I was trying to get details out of her past, she would shut down, being very careful not to escalate my jealous state. This caused emotional walls and barriers to be erected early in the relationship. These walls blocked much of our true potential connection. Not a day went by that I wasn't obsessed with one of her exes. She would try to pry so far back into her history that even she couldn't remember the details of her past. I would put the imaginary puzzle pieces together for her and create my film reels, ready to loop in the Retroactive Jealousy movie theater in my head. Anything she said would be mentally noted down and used against her. As our fights became more frequent, they escalated to the point of almost breaking up. The thought of breaking up offered me an intense sense of relief, as I would no longer have to think about her past and would be able to let her go. In truth, I was trying to let go of the past I had conjured up in my head, not her. I wasn't conscious enough at the time to realize that if I left the relationship, the relief would be very, very short-lived. I can be free from RJ for a certain period. But, as I embarked on a new relationship in the future and those familiar and exciting feelings came flooding back, so did my RJ triggers, the despair, and all the nightmarish drama that went along with it. I thank heaven they paired me with someone so strong inside of her that she wouldn't leave me and promised to work with me no matter how bad it got, even when I proclaimed that I would never get better (it can feel that way when I suffer from RJ). If your partner is not so understanding, don't be afraid. The problem is not theirs; you must transform from within, regardless of any external support system or the involvement of a loved one. The problem wasn't with Sarah, the problem was deep inside me. I had to get to the core of my pain. Why was I so worried about these guys from her past? Why did I care so much about the details of these men to the point of unhealthy obsession? The journey in search of these answers led me to discover a lot about myself, including who I was and what I wanted in life. But first, I needed to not only master the pain so I could see clearly enough to grow, but I needed to dig into the root of my pain and rip it out with both hands. Over time, with a lot of self-reflection, and hard work, I was able to improve. Since then, I have never been happier.

My healing journey began with the aforementioned epiphany that the way I was acting was not right, nor conducive to any kind of enjoyable life for myself or my partner. This led to an extensive online search in which I tried to collect as much information as I could about any jealous patients who had symptoms similar to mine. It was then that I made the revolutionary discovery that this type of jealousy had a name: Retroactive jealousy. Up to this point, I had simply referred to my behavior as simple jealousy. As you've probably already found out for yourself, RJ isn't just boring old jealousy. Finding out that I was not alone was enormously comforting. I found some helpful resources and even discovered an RJ patient Facebook group! However, I found a lot of counterproductive and insensitive information and "help" online, which was not produced by someone who had suffered from RJ. Some articles offer useless nonsense like "your past doesn't matter; you just need to get over it; everyone has done something." As you've probably discovered, this kind of advice is a fleeting relief at best, and will probably spark you off quickly thereafter.

As I discovered more and more about RJ and patients around the world, a new sense of fighting spirit and optimism came over me that told me, "This can be done! I can get through this!" Before this moment, I had proclaimed the same old broken-record statement of "I'll never get better." As you speak, so you will be. I started to change this inner language very quickly. Reversing my negative self-talk was a great ally in my recovery. As I became more aware of my emotions and behaviors, I began to question all aspects of my emotional state. Through much reading and study, I began to understand more about myself. One of the areas of myself that I became aware of was my intense fear and nervousness when out in public at night. I had always experienced these feelings, but they were always below the surface and I was not aware of them. As I delved into why I felt this way, memories of violence inflicted on me by older children in my youth began to surface. I started seeing a therapist recommended by a relative. During my work with the therapist, I discovered that these subsurface feelings of fear and stress were affecting much of my life, not just when I was out in public at night and felt vulnerable. Without knowing it, I carried the emotional scars and fear inflicted on me as a child into my adult life. This discovery made me realize why I felt so weak and small compared to my partner's exes (whom I had imagined and told myself were stronger, taller, and generally more physically impressive than I was). Everything began to come together piece by piece. My fear, my weakness, my sense of vulnerability. It all stemmed from my simple case of insecurity. If I had experienced scenarios in my youth where I had felt and seemed strong, brave, and heroic instead of weak and downtrodden, I probably would have carried this into my adult subconscious mind, and perhaps RJ would never have inhabited my being. It became clear that much of what I suffered as an adult was a direct result of certain experiences in my youth. I had to correct these unhealthy subconscious habits that were bringing me down. Later, I will get in touch with my inner child.

A book that helped me achieve healing of this inner child was "Healing the Shame That Binds You" by John Bradshaw.

I had discovered that many of my adult insecurities stemmed from the fact that, deep down, I felt weak, small, and vulnerable. This was a great discovery as it meant that I now knew what I was working with. I could fight my problem with its polar opposite. If I felt weak, then I had to find a way to feel strong. If I felt shame, I had to fight this with confidence. If I felt fear, I had to fight it with courage.

I am providing this information in the hope that you will look deep within yourself to discover exactly what it is that makes you feel so insecure. It probably comes from your youth. I recommend you find a therapist who helps you get to know your inner child. Probably, some life experiences have caused you to become an adult who is not comfortable with yourself; an adult with insecurities powerful enough to conjure a beast like Retroactive Jealousy. I eventually worked on my weakness issues by joining a Muay Thai class (and becoming a fighter), joining a gym, and retraining my subconscious mind to replace negative self-talk with affirmations of confidence and power.

With a lot of fresh research in my mind, a wonderful therapist, and a new understanding of myself, I had many areas in which to begin my healing work. After approximately 18 months of dedicated, strategic, and relentless transformational work, I was free of RJ's insidious control. Triggers often kept trying to get my attention but to no avail. I was too good at ignoring triggers. I was too good at focusing on the positive and my mind was busy with wonderful life-affirming thoughts and activities. Now, sometime later, I am 100% free of triggers, intrusive RJ thoughts, and all the destructive drama that goes along with them. You can be too! My relationship has never been better.

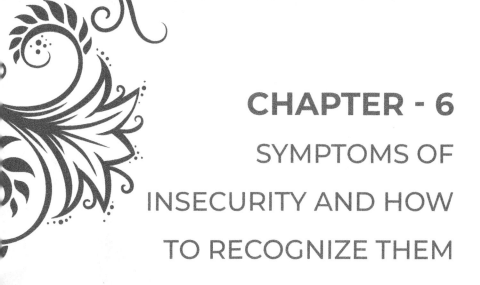

CHAPTER - 6

SYMPTOMS OF INSECURITY AND HOW TO RECOGNIZE THEM

Blaming the Other

I f you're always nagging or blaming your partner for everything, you need a rude awakening. This happens when your ego controls your relationship and uses manipulative tactics to do so. Do you ever take responsibility for your actions? Would you be able to move aside and think from another perspective without accusing the other person? The ego will want you to find fault and scrutinize the mistakes of others. You will do everything and anything to blame and criticize another person. Surprisingly, what we avoid is usually what we end up receiving in our relationships. If you don't take responsibility for yourself, your ego will help you project all of this onto your partner.

Playing the Victim

Is it safe to say that you are playing the unlucky victim card in your relationship? Do you always compare yourself to your partner? Is it true that you are continually putting yourself down? An unhealthy ego will help you reinforce negative actions instead of positive ones. It will make you focus too much on your imperfections. If you're doing this, it's time to venture out and take another look at your relationship. You are not a saint.

The time has come to be responsible for what you bring to the table and stop constantly blaming your partner for everything.

Being Jealous

Jealousy is the green-eyed monster, and it usually sets the stage for negative drama in a relationship. The ego tends to feed on self-esteem and lack of recognition. A loving relationship depends on the consideration and awareness of each other. Love does not contribute to comparing, belittling, and criticizing as the ego does. This is a show that turns into the most amazing kind of negative drama in any relationship. If you are in an abusive relationship, your ego will not let you go out of jealousy. What makes you consider these ideas? Does your partner make you question the validity of your relationship? This means that you need to venture back and be forthright in identifying the abuse in the relationship.

Fearing Rejection

This type of fear prevents you from moving forward and achieving any of your goals. When you stop as a result of this fear, you are unfair to your relationship. Changing the way you perceive things instead of being incapacitated by anxiety and upset caused by your ego will be a healthy way to boost self-esteem. Negative self-talk will only feed your ego. Don't compromise who you are to give in to your partner's ego. This is anything but healthy. A loving relationship depends on mutual respect and recognition. If you feel rejected, it might be time to reevaluate your relationship.

Always Having the Last Word

Your ego takes every little thing about you and turns it into a one-person game. If you find that you talk about yourself a lot and don't ask about your partner, well, you're immensely ego-driven. The ego plays an excellent role in protecting us from achieving total harmony and joy. It is the mind's method of control. It will also create situations in your mind that do not exist. If you find that you need to call the shots on all things, it's time for you to venture out and discover the root of this need. Do you feel you are better than others or second rate? Do you lack self-confidence and need to prove yourself worthy despite all the problems in this way? The ego will make you hide your sense of mediocrity by overvaluing yourself. If you and your partner fight a lot, your ego is likely fueling these fights. Is this how you feel important in your relationship?

It's important to step back and look at your relationship at times. You need to identify when you are the one who is wrong and making mistakes. Take a look at your actions and recognize when they are ego-driven. You have to put your ego aside if you want a strong and healthy relationship with your partner.

If you have a big ego or your love is selfish, what should you do? For the narcissist, being right all the time is deeply connected to his sense of self-worth. In this way, individuals who cannot give up their egos do and say what they want and always think they are right. Tragically, this will come at the expense of many other things. Your need to always be right can cost you relationships with colleagues, supervisors, family members, and in most cases, your partners. Sooner or later, you have to understand that the false self-esteem you get from clinging to your ego and "being right" doesn't outweigh genuine happiness.

Being true to yourself and practicing mindfulness will allow you to understand that you cannot be right in all circumstances. There will be certain situations where you make a mistake, have the wrong mindset, or are essentially on the wrong side.

It can be hard to admit this at times; however, having the ability to concede when you mess up can be quite liberating. Take responsibility for your actions and decisions, and soon you will see the ball will be in your court!

You don't have to be better or bigger than everyone around you. The need to be like this can be quite destructive for you. A great sense of ego leads you to believe that you are superior to anyone else. It's similar to remembering that you don't need to be right all the time. Understand that you don't have to be better than others either. That is not a healthy level of competitiveness for anyone. There will always be someone better, prettier, smarter, faster, and richer than you. No matter how old you are, this will always be the way of things. The sooner you understand that you cannot—and should not feel committed—to being superior to other people, the sooner you can repair and improve your relationships.

Instead of competing with others in this regard, why not consider improving yourself? You are perfectly unique. Focus on how you can improve, and each of your relationships will improve.

- **Exercise:** It is essential to see how activity impacts both the body and the mind. When you work out regularly, your body releases endorphins into your circulatory system, which improves your mood. Also, your psyche will be occupied by restless musings. It is known that exercise helps our general mood and decreases signs of nervousness and sadness. As physical exercise increases, your anxiety lowers. Some engaging activities that have been explicitly linked to helping with tension include yoga and judo. This is because these activities help individuals be careful in their development and center while clearing their brains. As you structure a daily practice with your activity, your body will begin to produce serotonin and endorphins before, during, and after the exercise. These artificial concoctions that are provided to the mind seem to diminish the melancholy and discomfort fundamentally. Training supports confidence, improves certainty, allows you to start feeling engaged and trustworthy, and helps you create strong new social connections and camaraderie.

- ***Start a healthy diet:*** The mind requires an enormous amount of vitality and sustenance to function effectively. Healthy nutrition can bring about huge changes in your physical health. A terrible diet means you are not providing the necessary supplements for the synapses in your mind to work effectively. In light of that, it could be worsening the manifestations of his nervousness. By following a healthy eating regimen and filling your plate with whole new foods, drinking the perfect amount of water, and making sure you're getting the right nutrients, minerals, and trans fats every day, you're giving your brain the right energy of food for battle ability and anxiety. A solid eating routine also involves dealing with your intestines and stomach tract. Remember that a good eating routine is to eliminate enhanced beverages such as iced teas, soft drinks, and natural blended juices. Studies have shown that people who drink a large number of soft drinks every day are more than 30% more likely to experience the harmful effects of nervousness and blues than people who don't. Sugar-free beverages like plain espresso, homegrown teas, and water-containing organic products are much more beneficial alternatives for keeping your body and brain hydrated. Caffeine is also a supporter of the side effects of stress and should be reduced to combat caffeine symptoms.

- **No more liquor:** Liquor is a focal sensory system depressant and is a known stress reliever; but as we all know, it is very harmful to our health. Some people try to mitigate the effects of their nervousness by drinking liquor; however, in reality, alcohol is often the basis of their tension. Liquor intrudes on sleep, dries out the body, and prevents a person from controlling current problems instead of facing and acknowledging the root and reason for their anxiety.

- **Catch up on your rest:** Poor propensities to sleep affect an individual's mood. This is because the synapses in the brain need time to rest and recharge to keep the mindset of the body stable. Legitimate eternal rest allows the brain to adjust hormone levels and makes a person more likely to adjust to her anxiety. The unfortunate propensities for falling asleep and sleep deprivation do not need to be modified with synthetic compounds. Terrible rest propensities can be corrected using standard techniques including melatonin, teas, home-grown blends, exercise, and contemplation. The moment you make sure you are getting a good rest, your mind will begin to address your hormone levels.

- **Start addressing your feelings:** This book covers managing your negative thoughts and moods in general terms and being restless works wonders for the body's hormones and powers the brain to create more synthetic concoctions to try and feel optimistic. Ultimately, the brain becomes exhausted and unable to produce the hormones that are expected to fight disease and stress. By preparing your psyche to consider reflection emphatically and pay close attention, you can shift your recognition of what is happening and begin to take responsibility for your negative considerations. By fighting back and silencing your negative contemplations, you can overcome your nervousness, ensuring that you are better prepared to bounce back in your relationship. Be sure to rehearse all kinds of positive confirmation, including apologizing, appreciating your life, and considering other people. The moment you can be positive, the restlessness begins to subside and you are better prepared to talk to your partner without bringing negative and silly behavior. Continually remind yourself that you are responsible for your life. If there are circumstances that make your tension explode, you can transform them.

- **Reduce your pressure:** Stress increases nervousness more than ever and triggers the body's fight or flight reaction. By learning techniques to manage pressure and control, by focusing on the factors, you are allowing your body to be more likely to deal with its normal reactions to what it sees as risk. By learning techniques, you will be able to handle immense pressure. Figuring out what's bothering you allows you to take the pressure off or create methodologies to help you deal with your pressure. Practicing relaxation systems, and reserving effort to revive and appreciate life are great ways to relax the mind and allow nervousness to ease. Become flexible to stress and realize that, little by little, you have power over pressure.

- **Reach out and locate a strong support base:** A strong

relationship begins with strong companionship. Having a decent informal organization that offers you support and a sounding board as you work through your stress is critical to healing. Restlessness can cause an individual to need to detach; However, a decent support structure means you'll always have someone to connect with when the stress recedes. They should be people who find the positives in you and can give you sensible and objective feedback when you talk about what is causing your discomfort. They should provoke you to look within yourself, and they should help you quiet that down. Make sure you maintain excellent and quality contact with your loved ones who make it like yourself. Do whatever it takes to not get involved with the pessimism of others. Try to volunteer to increase your point of view in your life and associate with other people who have problems with emotional well-being. If you're not yet at the point where you need to see a counselor, try joining a care group. Consider hugging a child to help calm their nervousness and show them unconditional love.

- **Find your motivation:** People who have a strong sense of their motivation can deal with pressure and nervousness better than people who don't. Finding your motivation gives you a boundary against the impediments your inner expert describes for you. Those with a strong sense of direction, in general, will find that life is much more fulfilling and they can see the positive qualities in every circumstance instead of stressing over how terrible it may be. Your motivation does not have to be a vocation or a leisure activity; find your other world, invest energy considering your qualities, volunteer on decks or non-profit associations, recognize and use your unique gifts to help other people, and recognize that life is about rhythmic movement: that should be your method to find your motivation. When you discover your motivation, you can become strong and fair with yourself, which allows you to be honest with your partner as well.

Using some or all of the systems set forth above is the way to beat nervousness in your relationship. Coping with your stress isn't just about seeking treatment. It's finding answers to a deal with your degrees of unease in a way that works for you and, ultimately, your partner. By understanding that your couple is not your adviser and taking responsibility for your stress, you will be better prepared to resolve the core issues that have caused your nervousness in any case. The moment you understand these central issues, you begin to take responsibility for your life again by working through your basic, unreasonable ruminations and replacing them with positive thoughts and activities. Although the tension can never be relieved, it can be done with changes in procedures and lifestyle. Having the option to silence your inner expert, talking to your partner, letting them talk to tune in with you, all allow you to change your lifestyle. It encourages you to take responsibility for your life again and improves your relationship. If you are involved with someone who is experiencing nervousness, we believe this book has helped you better understand what stress is, what causes discomfort, and how to help them help heal and deal with their tension. For people who are enduring concerns, we trust that, by reading this book, you have had the choice to empower yourself and take the steps you hope to begin to improve your satisfaction and your relationship. Therefore, taking responsibility for your stress and choosing to work with it will allow you to personalize your journey to healing yourself and your relationship.

CHAPTER - 7

HOW TO OVERCOME INSECURITY IN A RELATIONSHIP

Relationships require maintenance and constant work for them to be successful and develop into a long, loving, and happy relationship. People are often taught that love just happens and sometimes even told that for a relationship to be successful, love is all that is needed. However, relationships are much more than that, and love is not enough. Love can be the first spark that ignites the relationship, and that is how it came to be. To build a lasting connection with another person, you need to think in more realistic terms when it comes to defining love. Expanding on the simplistic vision, or fairy tale, that you dreamed of when you were young is the first step.

For a happy relationship, you have to actively work on it and make the best of everything you find on your way to happiness. Having a happy relationship means making conscious decisions that will contribute to that happiness, even if sometimes the decisions you make seem challenging.

Everyone makes mistakes when it comes to relationships, and we're not just talking about romantic ones. Even with friends, our behavior can influence how much they trust us, how much we connect with them, and on what level. Just because we all make mistakes doesn't mean there's nothing you can do about it. There is a lot! There are actions that both you and your partner can take to avoid mistakes; know how to handle them if they have already happened, and bring happiness to your relationship:

1. **Your partner is your equal:** This is something that people often forget when they are bossing each other around. Do you recognize yourself or your partner while reading this? Instead of being the leader of the relationship, try to collaborate. Work together, listen to your partner, and be as supportive as possible.

2. **Be respectful:** Spending a lot of time with just one person can be exhausting, especially if you live with your partner. Sometimes it may seem like your partner is triggering your nerves or anxiety and you may feel anger or resentment building. You may end up lashing out even if he or she is not entirely to blame. No matter how you feel or how angry you are, your partner needs to learn about such emotions, respectively. Communication plays an important role here, as well as self-control. Practice both even outside of your relationship, and you will only see the positive influence it leaves on people.

3. **Spend quality time with your partner:** When your relationship was fresh and new, you spent a lot of time together and did everything together. Where did all that go? Well, life happens, children arrive, people focus on their jobs and careers, home, homework, etc. Some may lose all the free time they used to spend with their partners. Still, for a relationship to succeed, you need to make that time even when it's scarce. Happy relationships demand

that you push yourself and your partner to do something together. It is not enough to talk to each other at the end of the day about work or various problems. Quality time means getting to work together on a project. For example, you can repaint your house, build a dollhouse for your children, go on a hike or exercise together, volunteer at an animal shelter, etc. Working together on something that interests you both will reconnect and even learn new things about each other. It is a satisfying and enriching experience.

4. **Learn to forgive:** Knowing how to forgive your partner's mistakes is essential, but you also have to be willing to forgive yourself. Empathy plays an important role in forgiveness. It helps you feel your partner's emotions, understand their behavior, and make room in your heart for real and unconditional forgiveness. Be the same with yourself. Learn self-compassion and practice it. It is a great skill that will not only heal the wounds created by mistakes but will also teach you not to

5. **Expectations:** When you commit to someone, it doesn't mean you should trust him or her to make you happy. Young couples often make this mistake. Your partner is your life partner and not just an accessory. Don't expect your partner to fully understand or know you, as this can rarely be done by just anyone and will only cause you various feelings of anxiety. Remember that you are two people, with their particular experiences, who are supposed to complement each other. He/she is not entirely responsible for your happiness. Just being with your partner should bring you relief and joy, and if you want more from your relationship, it's up to you to make it happen. If there

is something your partner could do that would make you happy, be open about it and say so clearly. People can't read minds, and relationships often fail simply due to miscommunication, which stems from having unclear expectations and making assumptions.

CHAPTER - 8

NEGATIVE THOUGHTS: HOW TO ELIMINATE THEM?

O ther people's complaints and problems are of little interest to anyone, and in most cases, if there is a problem, then you have to solve it. A man is the blacksmith of his life, and if there are any questions, you must solve them yourself, because no one will help a person better than himself or herself.

If you constantly go through your problems, this leads to the fact that the negative accumulates and, as a result, climbs sideways in the form of illnesses. If you do not want to be treated later, mentally prevent future illnesses, that is, stop thinking about insoluble situations and simply solve them.

To get rid of the discomfort within yourself, without deciding the cause of the discomfort itself, you can simply pronounce it if it is important, whether it is a girlfriend, a stranger, or just walls. This (not effective) method of temporarily getting rid of spiritual discomfort is beneficial only to the individual himself, but the problem remains a problem, while the person to whom you have entrusted your adversities will in any case have an opinion about you that will be constantly designed, whether you want it or not. Dissatisfaction with themselves and with life can become the reason why people inadvertently begin to ruin their lives and that of their associates, and the time that could be spent on solving a specific problem is wasted on talking.

If you see that the person with whom you decided to talk is trying to get away from the conversation and has a disgusted face, it means that you are doing something wrong, and now the question arises, was it worth starting the conversation? Of course, the interlocutor may have many reasons for the upset person, but you do not need to be selfish and constantly talk about your sorrows because a normal person who constantly listens to pity will begin to get bored, in general, lose interest, and eventually try to avoid the conversation as such for some reason altogether. People like to hear positive information more, and the point is not even flattery, but the fact that by hearing positive information, even the mood improves, and it is much more pleasant to communicate with a positive person than with a weeping individual.

As a result, some people try to calm down while talking about a problem, but without solving it, while others, on the contrary, act and get rid of it. It turns out that talking in vain does not lead to anything; it only gives a calming effect for a time and does not do more; therefore, "talking about the problem" is not a method to solve it.

How do you find a way to solve life's problems? Alas, there are no universal options because each case is individual, but there is an interesting algorithm of actions to which you can get closer to the goal. The first thing to do is to compose by yourself in your mind or write on a piece of paper several ways to resolve a controversial situation.

If you didn't manage to solve the problem, try to find more ways to solve it; if it's half solved, then this is the result, you tried, but if you figure it all out by yourself and get a negative or positive answer, you can be calm, because there is a result.

Your problem is in the past, and you begin to spend your time and health vigorously thinking like this: "what if" and so on. It is necessary to stop because such self-digging will not lead to anything; history is already in the past; we must think ahead and act. Engage in physical labor and it will distract you and bring its results, and finally cheer you up.

Learn to see yourself from the outside, developing a high level of self-control, because only in this case will you stop digging into the past and thinking about the negative. Life energy does not need to be wasted thinking about what would happen if it were too destructive. You need to tune into the positive; even if the negative doesn't get out of your head, find something good around you and make it the center of your thoughts.

To avoid destroying yourself inside, tune in to positive thinking because you must have the self-preservation instinct.

The internal state of a person depends solely on him/her, so you should focus on the positive. You managed to prepare yourself for the positive, but what if people with negativity surround you? Yes, you can't escape some situations, but if you learn to develop a positive attitude (if you haven't developed it since childhood, you can minimize the negativity you get from talking to him/her). People who only think about the bad situations have always existed and will exist, and this is a fact, and you have to treat them calmly (unless, of course, you have the strength to listen to something negative constantly) and let all that go. To think positively, you need to work long and hard on yourself, both emotionally and physically, while often overdoing it in laziness.

Negative information is completely useless; it's destructive, so you have to make sure it gets past you. If you can't listen to your negative-minded interlocutor, limit the time and opportunity to communicate with them and subtly hint that you are more interested in other topics of conversation. Bring the thought to the speaker on an abstract level that bad thoughts are reflected in real life and are the cause of failure.

If you want to help your friend, offer him or her several options to solve their situation, and if they ignore your recommendations, simply move the conversation to another topic since it is clear that the person is not interested in solving the problem but simply wants to complain, and we know that such talks lead nowhere.

Therefore, we conclude that to stop thinking about the negative, you need to regularly work on yourself while trying as little as possible to focus on the undesirable and think about the good. It is not necessary to focus attention on the adverse situations in your life; try to forget all this quickly. At the same, time understand that thinking about painful situations can harm your body.

A positive attitude is an essential companion to an active lifestyle. If a problem has arisen, it is necessary to clearly and quickly accept it as it is and outline an action plan for its elimination, proceed with its implementation, not forgetting to spend at least 2 hours a day in the fresh air. Additionally, go into your daily routine, and start doing gymnastics or any other physical exercise.

Have You Had to Deal With Negative People?

If so, then you know it can be difficult. I remember my old coworker who was like that. During our conversations, he constantly complained about his colleagues, work, and life.

However, she spoke very cynically about people in general, constantly doubting his intentions. Talking to her was not a pleasure. Absolutely. After our first conversation, I felt completely drained. Even though we only talked for 20 to 30 minutes, I didn't have the heart or the strength to do anything else.

I had the feeling that someone had sucked the life out of me, and this effect took about three hours to wear off. When we spoke later, the same thing happened. I was so pessimistic that her negative energy seemed to wash over me after the conversation and even left a nasty aftertaste in my mouth.

And you know, she pissed me off. I would gladly refuse to communicate with her if I could. Then one day, I decided that I needed to develop a plan of action: how to deal with negative people. In the end, she is not the only person I have met in my life. I thought: for every negative person I know now, there will be thousands of people I can meet one day. If I learn to cope with it, I can cope with everyone else.

With this in mind, I brainstormed the best way to deal with negative people. In the end, I found some key tricks to do this effectively. They can be very helpful in building good relationships with those persons. And even though I deal more often with positive people now, these steps come to the rescue when I sometimes run into negative individuals.

If there is such a negative person in your life now, you don't have to suffer for it. You are not alone in her problem—I often met negative people and learned how to deal with them. Let them try to humiliate you—you can choose how to react and what to do. These tricks work for me and they can certainly help you deal with people like that.

Don't Let Deny

I noticed that negative people tend to focus on the bad things and ignore the good points. They exaggerate the problems they face, and therefore, their situation seems much worse than it is. The first time you communicate with a negative person, listen carefully and offer help if needed. Be supportive—let them know they are not alone.

However, make a mark somewhere. If a person continues to complain about the same problem even after several discussions, it is a sign that they need to break free. For starters, try changing the subject. If he or she gets into a negative corkscrew, let them continue, but don't get involved in the negative.

Give simple answers like "Yes, I see" or "Yes." When they respond positively, reply affirmatively and enthusiastically. If you do this often enough, you'll soon understand what's going on and become more positive in communication.

Using Groups to Talk to a Negative Person

When I talked to my negative colleague, I was completely exhausted for several hours, although the conversation itself lasted only 20 to 30 minutes. This was because I took on all the negativity from him. To solve this problem, let someone else be with you when you are talking to a negative person.

The more people, the better. Then the negative energy will be shared between you and other people, and you won't have to bear its gravity alone. A bonus of someone else being around— other people help to identify the different sides of the individual. When there are others around, they can help to discover a different and positive side of the negative person. I had experienced this before, which helped me see the "negative" personality more positively.

Objectifying Comments—Negative People Can Be Quite Critical at Times

They periodically throw out comments that can hurt, especially when directed at you. For example, I had a girlfriend who was not very tactful. She loved to give various dismissive and critical comments. At first, I was worried about her words, wondering why she was so judgmental every time she spoke.

I also thought that maybe something was wrong with me, maybe I was not good enough. However, when I saw her communicate with our mutual friends, I realized that she behaved in the same way with them. Her comments were not personal attacks—this was her usual behavior.

Recognize that a negative person usually doesn't want to hurt you, they're just caught up in their negativity. Learn to deal with negative comments and objectify them. Instead of taking the words personally, consider them from another point of view. Drop the shell and see if you can benefit or learn from what is being said.

Switch to Nicer Topics, Some Negative People Start on Certain Topics

For example, a friend becomes a "victim of circumstance" when it comes to work. No matter what he says, he will keep complaining about a job where everything is horrible, and he won't be able to stop. If a person is deeply rooted in his negativity in her problems, a change of subject may be the solution.

Start a new topic to cheer yourself up. The simple things—movies, daily incidents, mutual friends, hobbies, and happy news can make the conversation a lot easier. Support him in areas where a person experiences positive emotions.

CHAPTER - 9
THE ATTACHMENT STYLE: WHY IT'S DANGEROUS, WHERE IT COMES FROM, AND HOW TO OVERCOME IT

The Origin of the Concept of Attachment

At the request of the World Health Organization (WHO), J. Bowlby made observations on the mental health of homeless children after World War II. From there, he concluded the capital importance of the need for a warm, intimate, and continuous relationship between the child and her mother figure. His studies highlight several psychological consequences for the child victim of deficiencies in maternal care, such as lack of intellectual concentration, inaccessibility to the other, or lack of emotional reactivity. In 1946, in collaboration with Robertson, Bowlby clarified his observations through research on the consequences of separation from the mother figure during infancy on the child's later development.

These authors observed that young children, deprived of their mother and admitted to a hospital or nursery, lived in profound suffering, which became more acute as the stay was prolonged. More precisely, his clinical observations allowed us to highlight three phases of visible and immediate reactions in children between six months and four years old before a separation: the protest phase, which begins with the departure and can last from a few hours to several weeks. It is a period in which children show deep discomfort and in which they try to use the available resources to recover their attachment figure. The second phase of despair informs a loss of hope of recovering the mother figure. The third phase is revealed by a detachment of the child, where the latter seems to reinvest the entourage. However, when the mother returns, the child does not show any behavior characteristic of attachment, as if motherhood and human contact no longer made sense.

These observations, sources of inspiration for Bowlby, led him to refute the drive-by libidinal oral satisfaction support theory developed by Freud to reconsider the notion of attachment to the mother. D. Anzieu (1996) refers to the 1958 article by J. Bowlby, The Nature of the Child Ties to His Mother, and speaks of "an attachment drive, independent of the oral drive and which would be a non-sexual primary drive." This theory, therefore, developed as a result of concern about the limitations and deficiencies of the child who suffered from the early separation and loss of parents after World War II.

Developed in 1958 by psychiatrist and psychoanalyst John Bowlby and inspired by the work of Donald Winnicott, attachment theory explores the foundations of relationships between human beings. According to Bowlby, the relational bases of each individual are forged and determined by the relationships experienced in early childhood. For a young child to experience balanced social and emotional development, he or she must be able to build an attachment relationship with at least one constant and ongoing caregiver. This attachment bond develops over the duration, availability, and quality of care.

It is through crying that the infant will express his requests, his needs, and his anxieties. The attachment figure can respond and appease. Bowlby refers mainly to the mother, who is more present in the first moments of life, but another adult referent is possible. The infant and attachment figures can then, if the relationship is harmonious and serene, refine their cry communication/ connection responses, leading to increased well-being. This attachment figure will become a secure base for the child that he can turn to if necessary, allowing him to explore the world.

How the attachment figure responds to the child's requests (crying) will therefore be decisive for the child's psychological and social development since it will guide the development of the child's attachment patterns that are essential for their future relationship. If the child receives a positive response to their requests, it is because he or she exists, which is why it is important. This individualization will allow him to evolve and develop positive family and social relationships. Generally, the child will become attached to adults who will be sensitive and caring.

During the 1960s and 1970s, developmental psychologist Mary Ainsworth developed Bowlby's attachment theory by adding the notion of "secure" or "insecure" attachment. It is from her field observations that Mary Ainsworth identified different types of attachments: secure attachments, anxious-avoidant (insecure) attachments, anxious-ambivalent or resistant (insecure) attachments, and disorganized (insecure) attachments. It is the quality of care that the child receives in early childhood (response to crying) that will determine the type of attachment that he develops.

The Attachment System: A Relationship Theory

The main goal of the motivational attachment system described by J. Bowlby is to establish physical proximity and comfort with the attachment figure. It is inspired by the model of control theory, born in mechanics, which defines behavior in terms of "established goals to be achieved, processes that lead to these goals, and signals that activate or inhibit these processes." (op. cit., p. 192) rather than in terms of tension and tension reduction, that Bowlby developed the concept of attachment.

The attachment system set in motion in the child allows them to maintain proximity with their attachment figure and its internal corollary: the feeling of security. Only when attachment needs are met can the toddler safely move away from their attachment figure to explore the world around them. This concept is innovative and is based on a theory of instinctive behavior. Bowlby (1978) posits that "the child's attachment to the mother is the product of the activity of several behavioral systems, the predictable result of which is the child's proximity to his mother." This attachment system has as its objective the protection and, therefore, the survival of the individual from an evolutionary perspective of adaptation.

In this sense, rather than a theory of the psychic functioning of the individual, attachment theory represents a conceptual framework that describes relational aspects and the need for security. According to Bowlby, once internalized, this bond of attachment would later serve as a model for all intimate and social relationships of the subject. From a more connectionist perspective, Guedeney (2002) defines this social and emotional bond as "the emotional connections between people when they are in an intimate relationship with others." This theory can be seen as a concept in which the internalization of the primary attachment bond represents a model for all relationships of the individual.

How Do Attachment Styles Affect Our Relationships as Adults?

We live in a time when it is increasingly difficult for us to build stable and satisfying relationships. Despite the emotional warmth we give, sometimes we find invisible walls beyond which we cannot penetrate. Or, on the contrary, someone is clinging to us and does not give us the right to privacy, claiming that this is true love. Every relationship carries with it the oldest pattern of affection—that of the baby with the mother. And this type of relationship is repeated indefinitely in our couples as adults. All of our stories of connection and separation matter.

The English psychiatrist and psychoanalyst John Bowlby (1907–1990) first attempted to organize early childhood experiences into mother-infant relationships. The first significant bond is between the baby and the person who cares for him. The child develops strong affective relationships with the person who cares for him. Bowlby's experience with hospitalized and homeless children in the 1940s shows him that a child needs closeness, warmth, and a constant relationship with the mother (or another caregiver) to develop normally. A newborn baby is so helpless that he cannot survive without the care and protection of an adult. In this way, the child builds behaviors that have the function of maintaining closeness with the person who cares for him. The attachment system is an internal program, part of our evolutionary heritage. When the closeness is broken, the child is in a state of intense anxiety.

There are three main attachment styles in early childhood—secure, anxious-avoidant, and anxious-ambivalent. The mother of children who build security always responds serenely to their emotional needs. She can hear her kid's emotions. They, in turn, freely explore the environment around them in her presence. Mothers of anxiously-ambivalently attached children are inconsistent with the infant's cues and are not always with them. Sometimes they are present, other times they are simply not available. These children, in an unknown situation, are "bats" for their mother. Children with anxiety-avoidant attachment styles were systematically hindered and their needs deflected. Mothers were often missing. These children do not even show separation anxiety. They are numb, focused on their toys, and not in contact with real people.

How do early attachment styles affect our mature relationships? Securely attached people will trust their partners; expect them to respond to their needs. Their relationships will be characterized by greater duration, trust, loyalty, and interdependence. They are more likely to use their partners as a secure base through which they dominate the world around them. People with an anxiety-ambivalent attachment style will constantly experience anxiety in their relationships about whether others love and like them. They will become easily frustrated and angry when their needs for closeness and affection are not met.

In the case of anxious-avoidant attachment, older adults will not be as involved in close relationships. On the contrary, they will prefer not to depend on others and for others not to depend on them. Individual differences in close relationships with adults depend on how comfortable they feel with closeness or avoidance and anxiety levels. Comfort with proximity is a strong sign of future satisfaction with dating partners. Anxiety reflects the degree to which the attachment system is activated in the presence of a threat from the environment or the connection. Typically, these individuals are overwhelmed by the idea of abandonment and the lack of satisfaction with their needs for attention and efficacy in the future, and at the same time, angry about the history of abandonment in the past (Bowlby, 1973).

Sometimes we are surprised by discrepancies. We heat and cool. We give security, and the people by our side do not believe they are loved. In those moments, let us remember that a whole world of attachment stories is based on the other. Sometimes without asking, they respond to them, not to us. But in time, we can tame this world with patience, perseverance, acceptance, and love.

Characteristic behaviors can be observed in children depending on the nature of the attachment:

In the case of a secure attachment, the attachment figure responds appropriately, quickly, and consistently to the child's requests. The attachment figure becomes a secure base for the child who will seek proximity in case of separation and will be reassured by the others, their presence. Secure children will be able to explore the world and fully develop their abilities.

In the case of attachment avoidance, the attachment figure responds little or not at all to the child's requests and values the child's exacerbated independence. The consequence of this detached response is the lack of emotional exchange and the introversion of emotions in the child. He/she is insecure, they do not understand, they do not calm down, and the child will not show signs of distress in case of separation or signs of appeasement when their attachment figure returns.

In the case of ambivalent or resistant attachment, the attachment figure offers an inconsistent and unstable response to the child's demands. The child is then lost and insecure. He/she will not be able to use their attachment figure as a base of security. They will show great stress during separations and will seek permanent contact with the attachment figure. Never reassured by the latter, the kids will live perpetually in fear of losing their love.

In the case of disorganized attachment, the attachment figure has a fixed, withdrawn, negative, and sometimes violent attitude towards the child. In response to this attitude, the kid will fear the attachment figure and, on occasions, will adopt an attitude similar to violence. The child is insecure. This type of attachment appears mainly in cases of domestic violence, mistreatment, abuse, etc.

CHAPTER - 10
THE FEAR OF ABANDONMENT

Fear of Abandonment: 10 Signs You Can't Ignore!

I f you want to get to the root of your abandonment issues and come out better on the other side, you'll want to pay attention to a few key points before moving forward.

1. Long History With Abandonment Issues

Abandonment issues are caused by a wide variety of different reasons, but not all of them necessarily have to do with choices you've made in the past. Many of them have to do with episodes you were exposed to throughout your life. As it turns out, one of the main signs you might have a fear of abandonment has to do with whether any of the following apply to you:

- You are the child of adoptive parents.
- You are the child of alcoholic parents.
- You have a long history of low or non-existent self-esteem.
- Your caregivers, whoever they may have been, were emotionally unavailable.
- Your parents divorced at a young age.
- You were abused at some point during your childhood.

- You have unfortunately lost a parent, a sibling, or both.

All of these important factors are major contributors to neglect problems that manifest later in life.

2. You Can't (Or Won't) Commit

Another major sign that you have abandonment issues is your commitment to relationships—or lack thereof. Many people think they make great romantic partners because they love the "newness" of a relationship. This is also commonly known as the "honeymoon period." However, once the honeymoon is over, you tend to find reasons to end things almost immediately.

This isn't necessarily the sign of a run of bad luck—it's a sign that you have abandonment issues that you need to work on.

3. No One Can Live Up to Your Standards

There's nothing wrong with trying to find perfection in a partner—as long as you don't let your expectations become too unrealistic. "Perfect for you" and "literally perfect" are two completely different things and should always be treated as such. Even people in the happiest, healthiest marriages you can find still have minor disagreements from time to time.

You should never let minor flaws make you break things, which is exactly what the fear of abandonment tends to do.

4. You Think Everyone Is Cheating on You

This is a particularly tricky subject, as it is not necessarily found in something fake. Infidelity is a very real thing, but if you constantly feel like every romantic partner you have is cheating on you, you're probably dealing with something else entirely.

You are afraid of abandonment problems caused by low self-esteem. If you find your justification for your suspicions, the idea of "of course, this person is cheating on me—why wouldn't someone cheat on me?" then the problem does not lie with others at all. It depends on you.

5. You Are Your Own Enemy

Another major sign that you have a fear of abandonment is when you can't seem to get out of your way and let your relationship develop on its own. Just when things are going well, you tend to screw things up.

Maybe you got into a fight over something small and insignificant. Maybe you did the unthinkable and cheated on your partner.

This doesn't make you a bad person—it makes you someone with a solution looking for a problem that needs to be solved first. You have the idea of "this is going to end badly eventually, so I'm going to end it now on my terms."

6. You Can Be Very Controlling

Being a bit on the controlling side in a relationship is one thing—being overly controlling to the point where you're essentially dictating how someone can live their life is something else entirely. To irrationally doubt every little move a person makes is not being in a relationship—it is being in a dictatorship. It is a major sign of distrust on your part, which in itself is one of the main signs that you have a deep-seated fear of abandonment that it is no longer healthy for you to ignore.

7. You Are Often Negative

Another of the main signs that you have a fear of abandonment starts along with the relationship itself. You meet a great new guy or girl who seems interested, but you can't help but immediately notice the flaws.

Some of them are small—he or she has an irritating voice or likes a movie that you think is horrible. Sometimes the details are big: you don't like what they do for a job or they have opinions you don't agree with.

The problem is that you are letting your thoughts act as barriers that will prevent you from getting more serious with the other person. All of this is based on the idea that you are so afraid of hurting yourself that you create these artificial "glitches" to stay ahead of the game.

This is also related to the unrealistic expectations you tend to set for potential mates, also known as the "Prince Charming" fantasy.

8. You Get Attached Too Quickly

One of the main signs that you have a fear of abandonment is if you instantly fall head over heels for whoever you meet. As soon as you meet someone, you're "in it for the long haul," even if you haven't had a chance to meet the other person in the first place. This isn't "love at first sight"; it's attachment, which is one of the main ways people with abandonment issues tend to sabotage themselves.

In his or her head, not only can they avoid abandonment by eventually being the one to abandon, but they also create their "get out of jail free" card. "I didn't do anything wrong," you tell yourself. "I was in this 100% from the beginning."

All you've done is find another effective way to end your romantic opportunities before they had a chance to take off in the first place.

9. You Never Allow Yourself to Get Attached

If you avoid becoming attached to a relationship, no matter how perfect the other person may seem, you are running into a long string of abandonment issues that you would do well to address for the good of everyone involved.

You can tell yourself that you don't want to get too serious so quickly. You can tell yourself that you value your single lifestyle and that you don't want to commit before you're ready. What you're doing is being emotionally uninterested, which is not how a healthy relationship is formed.

10. Your Fear of Abandonment Is Not Only Related to Your Romantic Life

Finally, if you want to identify signs of abandonment issues, look outside of your romantic activities. Let's say you're unsatisfied with your job and you want to make a change, but you never put in the effort to polish that resume because the "interview process is a hassle."

Maybe that's true, or maybe you don't want to apply for a job because you don't want to be rejected.

Maybe you're creative and just had an idea for a great short story. However, you never get down to business because you are fearful people won't like it. "It's better if it just lives inside my head," you think. "That is easier."

Or, you don't want to face possible rejection on the way to posting that story.

The point is that the fear of abandonment rarely exists in a silo. It doesn't affect only one area of your life (like your romantic life) while leaving other areas unscathed. It tends to affect everything about the life you are living, often for the negative.

If you start looking beyond your romantic relationships and see signs of abandonment and rejection issues, guess what, it might explain a thing or two about your ex-girlfriends or ex-boyfriends as well.

Again, none of this is to say that you are incapable of love or that you are somehow "broken." If you are, everyone else is too. What this means is that you are aware of the artificial barriers you are creating for yourself, particularly when it comes to your romantic pursuits.

If the first step to recovery is admitting you have a problem, simply recognizing these warning signs puts you in the best possible position to do something about it

How Will Fear Affect My Relationships?

One might think that this fear would go away once we get into a committed relationship. However, this is usually not the case. Those fears can manifest in ways where the person firmly believes that their partner will leave them and that it's just a matter of when, not if. They live every day worrying about being abandoned and not being able to give all to their relationship. They accuse their partners of cheating or trying to leave them.

They firmly believe that their partner is just waiting for the moment to walk away from the relationship. They feel that they cannot trust their partner's word, as their trust has been broken by others in the past.

However, they don't blame themselves and usually don't see how they contributed to the ultimate demise of their relationship. They simply believe that they are "doomed" in a relationship, that they are "unfriendly," and that everyone in their life leaves them without explanation. Therefore, without having this insight, the issues at hand will not be rectified and they will move on to the next relationship and continue these struggles.

Can This Affect Other relationship?

The answer is yes. Most people who have a fear of abandonment experience the same attitude towards other people around them, not just with a romantic partner. Instead, this could be with their parents, friends, and children. Typically, these fears manifest throughout a person's childhood. There is a parent who is absent from home or may leave home suddenly and without notice. When this happens, that child feels abandoned. However, if this father also comes and goes throughout the child's life, he or she may be afraid to trust that the father will stay because he leaves just when they begin to believe that he is going to stay.

Fast-forward a few years to the teens, and then you have someone who has the potential to be a very clingy friend. They may want to always be around their friends and get angry if a friend makes a new friend out of fear that they will be left behind. Now, if those friends know his or her family history, they can understand this attachment, but it can also become annoying. If that's the case, they can end the friendship. That would become a loss and, for that teenager, it would show that someone else just left them. Without having an idea of how they contributed to that, the cycle will continue.

Now, in their adulthood, they are in and out of relationships on this very topic. They become involved with a person whom they have difficulty trusting and who they believe will leave them. Therefore, they are afraid to approach them, and they are afraid to love them. Unable to reciprocate the feelings, the partner leaves. They continue without taking responsibility for the fall of yet another relationship and the cycle continues.

Unfortunately, this can continue for all the relationships in a person's life until they can finally realize that they may be contributing to this cycle of "their lives." Indeed, they couldn't control their parents' behavior, but recognizing that this is where these feelings started and they don't need to continue is the key. Once this is realized, the rebuilding can begin and they can live a happy and healthy life with a life partner in hand.

Effect on Relationships: An Example Scenario

1. Getting to Know Each Other Phase

At this point, you feel relatively safe. You are not yet emotionally invested in the other person, so you continue to live your life while enjoying time with your chosen person.

2. The Honeymoon Phase

This is when you decide to commit. You are willing to overlook potential red or yellow flags because you get along so well. You start to spend a lot of time with the other person, you always have fun, and you start to feel safe.

3. The Royal Relationship

The honeymoon phase cannot last forever. No matter how well two people get along, real life always intervenes. People get sick, have family problems, start working hard hours, worry about money, and need time to get things done.

Although this is a very normal and positive step in a relationship, it can be frightening for those with a fear of abandonment, who may see it as a sign that the other person is moving away.

If you have this fear, you are probably fighting with yourself and trying too hard not to voice your concerns for fear of appearing clingy.

4. The Light Relationship

People are human. They have weaknesses, moods, and things on their minds. Regardless of how much you care about another person, you cannot and should not expect that person to always be at the forefront of your mind. Especially once the honeymoon period is over, an apparent snub is inevitable. This often takes the form of an unanswered text message, an unreturned phone call, or a request for a few days of alone time.

5. The Reaction

For those with a fear of abandonment, this is a turning point. If you have this fear, you are probably completely convinced that the snub is a sign that your partner no longer loves you. What happens next is determined almost entirely by the fear of abandonment, its severity, and the sufferer's preferred coping style.

Some people deal with this by becoming clingy and demanding, insisting that their partner proves their love by jumping through hoops. Others flee, rejecting their companions before they are rejected. Still, others feel the snub is their fault and attempt to transform into the "perfect partner" in a quest to keep the other person from leaving.

In reality, the snub is most likely not a snub at all. Simply put, sometimes people just do things that their partners don't understand. In a healthy relationship, the couple may recognize the situation for what it is—a normal reaction that has little or nothing to do with the relationship. Or you may feel upset about it, but you deal with it with a quiet discussion or brief argument. Either way, a single perceived slight does not become a dominating influence on a partner's feelings.

6. The Partner's Point of View

From your partner's point of view, your sudden personality change seems to come from the left field. If your partner doesn't suffer from fear of abandonment, they probably don't have the slightest idea why their previously confident, laid-back partner is suddenly acting clingy and demanding, smothering them with attention.

Similar to phobias, it is impossible to simply talk or reason with someone out of fear of abandonment. No matter how many times your partner tries to reassure you, it just won't be enough. Eventually, your inconsolable behavior patterns and reactions could drive your partner away, leading you to the conclusion that you fear the most.

Coping Strategies

If your fear is mild and well-controlled, you may be able to control it simply by learning about your tendencies and learning new behavioral strategies. However, for most people, the fear of abandonment is rooted in deep issues that are difficult to resolve alone.

While dealing with the fear itself is essential, it is also necessary to develop a sense of belonging. Instead of concentrating all your energy and devotion on one partner, focus on building a community. No one can solve all our problems or satisfy all our needs. But a solid group of several close friends can play an important role in our lives.

Many people with a fear of abandonment say they never felt like they had a "tribe" or "pack" when they were growing up. For whatever reason, they always felt "other" or disconnected from those around them. But the good news is that it is never too late. Whatever your current stage in life, it's important to surround yourself with other like-minded people. Make a list of your current hobbies, passions, and dreams; then find others who share your interests. While it's true that not everyone who shares an interest will become close friends, hobbies and dreams are a great springboard for building a strong support network. Working on your passions also helps develop self-confidence and the belief that you are strong enough to tackle anything life throws your way.

CHAPTER - 11
WHAT IS JEALOUSY?

A little jealousy adds a bit of spice to a relationship, but too much jealousy can be destructive. Jealousy occurs when a spouse feels threatened by a third party that he or she believes to be a rival and a threat to their relationship. It can be healthy or harmful and can be based on real or just imagined threats. Unhealthy jealousy, which is often unnecessary and unreasonable, can ruin a marriage.

When Does Jealousy Become Unhealthy?

Jealousy is healthy when it pushes couples to be more loving, more sensitive, and committed because they value each other so much that they don't want to lose their partner. Unhealthy jealousy, on the other hand, makes the relationship problematic. Unhealthy jealousy or unnecessary accusations of infidelity push the jealous spouse to think and act irrationally. Extreme jealousy can push a spouse to have foolish thoughts and display unacceptable behaviors, which include stalking the accused spouse and going through and monitoring the partner's personal belongings such as phones, clothes, bags, diaries, social media accounts, etc. For example, you land with the workplace, what is found in the workplace, what must be done, and the worst of those who promise to make the accused confess.

Whether you are the jealous partner or your spouse is the jealous one, irrational jealousy can eventually destroy your marriage. Here are answers to frequently asked questions about jealousy and things you can do to overcome it in your marriage.

What Do Jealous People Feel?

Jealous people experience a multitude of feelings, including fear, anger, humiliation, failure, suspicion, threat, hurt, worry, envy, sadness, doubt, and loneliness.

Jealousy keeps us under a disheartening sense of frustration and disappointment. It makes us sad. It's such a depressing feeling that we can't even tell our best friends about it or contain it within ourselves. Consequently, it leaves us with the inconvenience of peculiar misery, and if allowed to grow unchecked beyond a limit, it functions as a slow poison to our healthy nature.

Dealing With Unhealthy Jealousy

As much as we'd like to deny it, most people struggle with jealous emotions at some point in their lives and, in marriage, it's one of those common problems that can develop from feelings of indifference. We now live in a society where marriages may not be the first relationship we've ever had. In some cultures, dating begins in adolescence, and second and subsequent marriages are common today. This is just society as we know it now. Insecurity often increases if a previous partner is still close, where one or both partners are consumed with social media, or where the couple lives separate lives (with one person away all the time working and socializing and the other yearning for a home and care). Overcoming insecurities and building self-confidence is something I frequently discuss in my online counseling sessions, for others it's simply letting go of jealousy.

If jealousy is affecting your relationship, here are some tips that have worked for my clients. The four most common triggers for jealousy that I see include flirting, infidelity, long hours at work, and the arrival of children.

If you're the one who's jealous, my heart goes out to you; it's a tough place to be. Common triggers are listed below, but for some I train, there are no triggers.

Jealousy Triggers

Long Working Hours

Too much time at work can make your partner feel very insecure, especially when your work hours increase and you spend less and less time at home for the sake of your family. Some may question whether it is really for the good of the family. It's not for me to judge, and you shouldn't judge yourself or your relationship unless it's causing a problem. Too often I see people become obsessed with their goals and have no idea how this affects their relationships and family life. This is actually what happened to me, I got so focused on my previous job goals and exercise regimen that I neglected my relationship and personal life. It is easy to do. I still can't believe I spent more than 14 hours a day exercising and working out, 6 days a week. If I loved my job, then maybe it wouldn't matter as much, but I didn't. So, it depends on your priorities and passion if you choose or need to work long hours. But if it's causing issues like jealousy, you may want to reassess and gain more balance. During long hours so that it is not a problem, both must see their benefits and make time for the connection.

Natural Flirting

Some people are natural flirts and notice good-looking persons when they walk into a room. Natural flirtations can often attract the opposite sex like magnets, which can leave the other insecure and simply waiting for the moment when they are dumped by the next person who shows up. The flirting partner often has no idea of the impact their actions have on their relationship. They don't believe they are doing anything wrong, but they perceive their actions to be friendly and not harmful. Yasser was a natural flirt, and Arwa couldn't stand it, she played so many scenarios in her mind, and it was affecting her sleep. We had a session where she agreed to check on him and show him more affection. I then spent a few sessions with her helping her not to take his behavior personally and to recognize that flirting doesn't mean he loved her less. She admitted that she married him that way, and she hoped that he might change after the marriage. In my experience working with many people, it's hard to change someone else, and part of loving someone is accepting them for who they are.

New Baby Arrival

Jealousy can arise if spouses feel abandoned when a new baby arrives, no matter how much they wanted the child in the first place. The mere existence of a baby is a total life change with more attention to the child and a complete 'dive in the nose' in marital relations. Since the bond between mother and child is so much closer (on average), it can leave the other feeling abandoned, unwanted, and a total spare part.

With some of my coaching clients, the jealousy around children worked the other way around. Katy felt trapped after the birth of her first child, and her husband David spent all his time taking care of the baby. She simply longed for their life before they had children when they traveled, enjoyed a good social life, and spent all their free time together.

No Trigger for Jealousy

While there are many other causes of jealousy, too many to mention here, there are also people I work with who tell me, "I know I have nothing to be jealous about, but I can't help it." "We are honest about everything. We share a joint email address, I have her Facebook password, and yet I can't help but think she's with someone else when I'm away from her, and I don't like it when she goes out at night without me."

Another client told me, "I know my jealousy is due to my insecurities about my appearance, my boyfriend is wonderful, and he understands, but I'm afraid I am driving him away with my obsessive mistrust." When there is no trigger, we need to see where it is coming from and take steps to increase our self-confidence and, more importantly, change our thought patterns.

Tips for Dealing With Jealousy

Jealousy in itself is not a bad thing, it is a strong indication that you care. The main point to remember is not to let jealousy consume, arouse anger and become destructive. If you are suffering from feelings of jealousy, then I have outlined some steps below:

Start by Questioning Yourself

Look at the cause, question your feelings and determine if they have any basis. Is your partner doing something wrong, has he really done something to fuel his jealous emotions, or has he just let his emotions get out of control? Then decide if it is you or their behavior that needs to change.

If This Is You, Calm Down

If you realize that maybe you are going overboard, my heart goes out to you. Most of us have been there at some point on some level. The fact that you recognize this is a big step. Does it come from past experiences? Is it tied to insecurities, fears of being rejected, or not having control?

Ask Yourself and Acknowledge Where This Is Coming From

Write your thoughts—getting them out of your head on paper or tablet can help.

Write a list of all the positive examples that the behavior could mean, for example—they haven't called because they can't or they're busy instead of "she's ignoring me because 'I think he' is with someone important at work; that's why that her coming home late is not about me, I promise not to take it personally."

Write a List of All the Reasons Trust Is Important to You and a Relationship

Focus your attention on yourself and something you like to do.

Have a list of friends and family you can call when a planned night or weekend doesn't happen, so you're not left with your thoughts wandering.

Write a long list of all the ways you know you're loved, big and small gestures.

Then, when you have episodes of jealousy, read the positive list, especially how you know they love you, and do an activity to distract yourself. Jealousy is caused by our thoughts, and the good point is that thoughts can be changed with practice and determination.

If You Think You Are—Please Contact

If you think there is something they are doing wrong, then communicate your feelings in a non-destructive way. Share your fears with your partner, explain how you feel, and seek their help so that you can overcome your jealous emotions. Think of some things you can do to make him or her feel more secure, whether it's calling more, taking an interest in his day, being more open with their thoughts, and asking them to do so. Don't forget to ask them about anything you can do for them as well. Use this as an opportunity to strengthen your relationship/marriage and build a stronger foundation for the future. Communication is the foundation of marital success. If you can learn to communicate, then you can express your emotions in a non-confrontational, non-accusing, understanding, and supportive environment.

Be careful not to blurt out your fears like "I think you're lying" or "I think you're having an affair." It may not be true and will only add fuel to the fire. Explain that something seems to have changed in your relationship, explain what has changed and what makes you think your marriage is different; don't blame, don't get angry, just explain to yourself and your partner what is going on to try to fix it.

One of the most common relationship problems is expecting our partners to always know what we want and how we feel. But even with a ring on our finger, we do not always mind readers, if we have not communicated our feelings and our partner does not know that, in our eyes, he has done something wrong, how do we expect him to do anything? About that!

If any of this sounds like you, then tell him or her how to improve your communication and marriage. You have everything to gain and nothing to lose. Even if the answer is not what you want to hear, knowledge is power, and with knowledge comes the ability to change your life.

CHAPTER - 12
WHAT ARE THE SYMPTOMS OF JEALOUSY AND HOW TO RECOGNIZE THEM?

We are jealous because, as we have seen, we are afraid that something, or someone, that we need to be happy will be taken away from us. What do you do when you experience it? Here are some points:

1. You check what the person you are jealous of is doing.
2. You try to impose limits that give you security (places, people, times).
3. You want to know what he or she did, where they were, and with whom. In short, you make sure you do what you think is right.
4. You tend to decide for the other person, imposing choices that give you security.
5. You want them to keep away from people you don't like, people you don't trust.
6. You start to fight, you crash, and there are moments of tension.

Am I Wrong?

You may have different ways of reacting to jealousy, but some, if not all of the things I've listed, are part of typical jealous behavior. Jealousy does not admit freedom because it is dangerous. They are exactly on opposite sides and never attract each other!

Think about it: jealousy means control, but also possession.

Are you jealous of my shoes, my girlfriend, or my TV? Of course not, these are my things, not yours. We are jealous of the things we consider ours.

Possession is, along with need, the basis of jealousy. You consider the people who should make you happy to be yours, and you feel jealous if you risk losing them. I give you good news: nobody belongs to you. You have no right to control a person. Wives, boyfriends, husbands, girlfriends, partners, call them what you want: they do not belong to you.

Jealousy is a form of mental travel. A jealous person starts having thoughts like, "If you go out with those people, I'll lose you." The very jealous man, in the group where other men are present, feels threatened and says: "If I'm not with you, you can't go out with those men because...." And so, begins the direction of his film, the mental journey that we are all good at doing. Everyone, without distinction!

Each person slowly falls in love with very interesting facts. A conscious person, however, then returns to the path of life. Another, on the other hand, gets stuck and messed up.

"I'm jealous because I love you too much and I'm afraid of losing you." This is the justification: is it so? Are love and jealousy related in this way? Does the person who loves so much make her love a "possession"?

The answer is no because where there is jealousy, there is love... but pathological! When jealousy and possession are exercised against the other, the choice to love gives way to imprisoned bars that can undermine the destiny of the relationship (as well as individual well-being).

You are imposing your presence and your possession in the life of the person you love. It can no longer be called love; more appropriate terms would be prison, possession, or any other word we want to use, but it is certainly not love.

We love a person when, together, we build a project with him or her and, at the same time, they remain free to move, breathless in the neck and respecting the other.

Jealousy can also break out in someone who feels immune to it if the loved one has, for various reasons, a singularity. In the eyes of the partner who has become jealous, that makes them precious and irreplaceable, almost a reason to live. A feeling that can explode, for example, when there is a strong difference in the feelings involved. When the other is perceived as "too much for me" because he or she is much younger, more beautiful, richer, more attractive, freer, and more courted. Jealousy, this intense negative emotion, is characterized by emotional pain, a sense of loss, and strong autonomic reactions, ranging from joy to anger, from excitement to tears.

What Causes Jealousy?

Why are you jealous of a person then? Allow me to generalize a bit, behind possessive jealousy hides the fear of being betrayed, of losing the person next to you, which, however, stems from a deep sense of insecurity. It is as if there is a belief that by finding a better person than you, your partner can walk away and leave you.

This is how the mask is revealed, that of wanting to be the perfect person, made for the other; however, it is an imposition, a directive that loses authenticity.

Jealousy breaks your mask so you can be seen for who you are:

a person, that is, who is on earth with other people's looks, even some better than you. They will always exist, and that is why my advice is to work on your sense of security to obtain the certainty of yourself, and not of your partner. The latter will never be enough to reassure you.

The term jealousy derives from Greek and means "ardor" and "rivalry."

The jealous person has an innate instinct to protect their partner, especially if someone or something compromises the balance of the couple. Being more exposed to jealousy is someone who has experienced moments of abandonment by parents. When the person in question becomes an adult, he or she has a constant need for attention, confirmation, and approval from those around him. Before someone who "does the splendid thing" with her partner or in a compromising situation, jealousy acts in favor of the union of the couple. His speech is determined and ironic. It makes its presence felt and is alert. This is a typical attitude of someone who has learned to balance their own emotional experience and make their partner feel protected and loved. In this case, jealousy is a form of attachment, synonymous with pure and true love.

The Ways Jealousy Changes People

Jealousy can become a form of selfishness and possession when it hides constant insecurity towards oneself and the partner in question. It can become pathological and is considered a threat to the relationship itself. Pathological or destructive jealousy becomes obsessive and generates extreme reactions in those affected. Pathological jealous people go crazy when they perceive a threat to the relationship. They say terrible things, they put pressure on the other, they are vindictive, and they fall into a pessimism difficult to manage and control. They can become dangerous and violent people.

To avoid jealousy ruining a relationship, here are our useful suggestions to handle it in the best possible way:

1. **Admit jealousy:** Becoming aware of it is the first step to maintaining a healthy relationship and learning to live with this uncomfortable feeling that can be a source of great suffering.

2. **Work on your insecurities:** Learn to accept yourself for what you have understood your defects that can contribute to making us unique and special to our partner. Stop making continual comparisons with other people. Suspend judgment and self-criticism.

3. **Constantly confront your partner:** Although it is difficult and, in some cases, even embarrassing to talk about this problem with your partner, it helps us understand the origin of insecurities. It is useful to plan concrete remedies and solutions together. This strengthens the agreement of the relationship.

4. **Do not make comparisons with the past:** Close once and for all with negative experiences related to previous stories. It is useless to reflect on the mistakes or grievances suffered. Focus solely on the current story, learning to trust the partner.

5. **Respect the spaces of others:** Change the attitude towards the individual spaces of the couple. Accept the fact that you have interests and passions. Do not try to cancel them but encourage them to cultivate what makes them feel good.

Jealousy goes hand in hand with open relationships but it can be the main obstacle in a relationship. It may seem contradictory because, after all, people who decide to start a relationship of this type seem to have overcome this feeling. In reality, however, very few people manage not to be jealous.

The problem is that many of the people who decide to have an open relationship, no matter how open they are and for personal freedom, do not take into consideration that jealousy can hit both them and their partner, and therefore, they are surprised when it happens.

Therefore, it is important to keep in mind that this problem could arise and accept jealousy, knowing that it can be overcome with the right strategies. Jealousy is a natural reaction, but when it is exaggerated, it can lead to irrational and harmful behavior.

Jealousy represents our fear of what we don't know and change, of losing power or control over a relationship, fear of loneliness and loss, as well as abandonment. It reflects our insecurity about our dignity, the anxiety about being adequate lovers, and the doubts about the appropriateness of our relationship.

Behind every feeling of jealousy, there is emotion much more important than jealousy itself. There is often an unfulfilled need or deep fear. Recognizing these fears and needs is the secret to unmasking our jealousy and nullifying its power over us.

Some people say that it is just a form of selfishness and possessiveness, others say that it is pure and simple attachment and that is true love, it should not be present. Others declare, on the contrary, that one cannot speak of true love without it. Very different opinions about jealousy have always converged. The truth is that it exists and is felt. In addition, it can show, depending on the case, two different faces, which can lead the couple towards two opposite destinations: one is the strengthening of understanding; the other is its progressive collapse. This is the reason why we can talk about constructive and destructive jealousy. They do not possess this protective instinct and, faced with an event that may arouse jealousy or even simple suspicion, they fall apart, and all hell breaks loose. They are no longer capable of reasoning or discernment and throw themselves at the partner, even when the partner has done nothing to encourage the situation. They go crazy: they say terrible things, they close themselves to all forms of intimacy and civic dialogue, and they threaten to end the story (children or no children, it doesn't matter), they magnify suspicions, they raise absolute vetoes, they pressure the other, they meditate revenge made of betrayals and fall prey to reckless pessimism. This reaction has only destructive power, leaving the couple in pieces. This type of jealousy is not "crazy."

The jealous party must accept having a long-standing effective problem and try to solve it; the partner must be patient and help the other to trust him, starting perhaps by not seducing in all fields.

1. **Constructive jealousy: a feeling that protects the relationship.** It is the ability to positively direct our own emotions in favor of the couple. When the bite of jealousy begins to be felt, the "constructive" jealous person reacts with greater interest in the couple, using the weapons of seduction and irony to strengthen the union.

2. **Destructive jealousy: an obsession built on insecurity.** It is the tendency to suspect that everything becomes obsessive for oneself and the couple. An obsession that poisons the relationship with unpleasant and blackmailing behaviors or with unjustified excesses. Here the primary interest does not seem to be the safeguarding of the couple but rather self-respect.

Here are practical tips for those who are too jealous:

Outside Help Needed

If the destructiveness of jealousy is high, it is necessary to learn less harmful behaviors, capable of extracting from these emotions the "passion" that can invigorate the couple. Targeted psychotherapy can be very helpful.

Try to Explain

Sometimes a scene is made because it is supposed to be accepted and there will be no consequences. But it's not like that. Do your best to explain your discomfort, suspicions, and annoyances to your partner. The effort to try to make yourself understood will be rewarded with greater self-confidence.

Practical advice for those who are jealous of others:

Stay Focused on Yourself

Don't trivialize what your partner says, don't let them go crazy, and don't react badly either. Instead, help them express their mood and calmly explain that there is no reason to be jealous.

Don't Be Seductive

If you stay with a partner who is so hypersensitive to the topic of jealousy, it's certainly not the case to go overboard with charm. Without giving up your natural self, avoid bi-directional teasing with the opposite sex in his presence, and don't make him feel neglected in front of others.

It is not easy; it's like a little monster slowly devouring your relationship. Both on the one hand and on the other, jealousy is terrible. If you are excessively jealous, you do not live well, you are always anxious about not having that perfect relationship that you would like so much. If instead, you are the part that suffers from jealousy, then you live in a real nightmare and never feel free to express yourself and what you want to do in your life and your relationship. Here it is very clear. Jealousy is not something you have to tolerate in your life. It is not something healthy, it is not an emotion that makes you feel good. No way. Eliminate this plague from your life.

The feeling of jealousy can be considered natural and normal when it is conscious, contained within the limits of individual perception, and expresses the understandable vulnerability that we all have when there is love, the idea of losing your loved one. It is also natural that it arises and causes suffering when the object of love is lost for the benefit of another. In such cases, the feeling of pain that accompanies physiological jealousy tends to diminish gradually. "Getting over it," as it is said in common language, indicates the healthy ability to overcome loss, to "cry," to respect the freedom of the other to leave and choose another object of love. This ability to accept abandonment, or at least farewell, presupposes maturity, inner balance, and confidence in our ability to love and be loved, as well as in our desirability. These feelings feed the trust and hope of being able to find a new object of love and to live a new nascent state of achievement, typical of someone who has lived primary relationships, in the family of origin, and in subsequent relationships, characterized by that certainty. and constancy of feelings that nurture secure attachment and self-confidence.

When It Is Extreme

Then we speak of delusional jealousy. This is associated with severe personality disorders and an increasing difficulty in controlling our destructive impulses. In these cases, the individual can become socially dangerous not only for the partner considered a cheater or guilty of abandonment but also for the same couple's family of origin or even for the children, as unfortunately reports all too often show.

CHAPTER - 13
WHERE DOES JEALOUSY COME FROM?

A s soon as you have realized that you are a jealous person, that this feeling affects you negatively, and that it is something that you would like to work on and change yourself, the next thing you have to do is an examination of conscience, get involved in introspection and learn things about yourself and what influences your behavior. Are you a jealous person in general? Or is it just a certain person that triggers your jealous behavior? Is your partner the one you can't trust? Or is it the other people? Do you feel threatened when members of the opposite sex approach your partner? Are you insecure about it? These are all questions to which you have to find an answer.

You may find that you have trust issues. This could be strictly related to your partner, or it could be a deeper problem you have with the opposite sex or in romantic relationships. Stop and think about why you don't trust your partner. It may be because he has disappointed you before or given you a reason to distrust him or because of a previous negative experience you had in a love relationship in which your trust was betrayed.

Most of the time, jealousy stems from the fear of losing the person you love. Consequently, members of the opposite sex that your partner finds attractive or have shown interest in may make you feel threatened by them, their presence, and their interactions with your partner. You may feel that he prefers this other person to you or is somehow better.

This ties directly into any feelings of insecurity you may be struggling with. Jealousy is an expression of deep insecurity in many cases, a feeling of inadequacy and inferiority. In your distorted understanding, the fact that your partner pays attention to this other person is a sign of a clear preference for the other over you, the one who loves him or her and is always there for the partner. Therefore, you may feel betrayed by these flirtations or innocent interactions and convince yourself that the other person is trying to steal your partner from you.

This type of behavior is the expression of innate jealous nature, not jealousy caused by external factors. However, jealousy can also be triggered either by your partner's behavior or by members of the opposite sex flocking to them and showering them with attention, leading to the insecurity and feelings of inadequacy we discussed earlier. Suddenly you are faced with all the options that are presented to your partner, and you begin to fear that they might choose someone else.

You must know the difference between the type of innate jealousy and those triggered by external factors because they are different situations that require different processes. A person who has a jealous nature needs to seek resolution within himself or herself and work on their mentality, psychology, and inner workings. A person whose feelings of jealousy appear only in certain situations, influenced by their partner's behavior, on the other hand, should talk to him or her about it and have an open discussion about how they feel and the role their partner's behavior plays in it.

As a person who is insecure and lacks confidence in himself or herself and their worth, they are bound to be the jealous type. This is because they are so convinced of their worthlessness that they perceive anyone else who interacts with their partner as a potential threat to their relationship and their happiness. Low or no self-esteem and an inferiority complex common in people like this can lead to the fear of being abandoned in favor of someone better, which is why you tend to protect your "turf," so to speak, more fiercely than others.

People whose jealousy stems from personal insecurity are the type who is constantly under the impression that they are being taken advantage of, cheated, outwitted, and betrayed. The insecure person doesn't want to be made a fool of and retaliates aggressively, with massive jealous behavior that can border on being controlling, possessive, and territorial. Constantly accusing the partner of cheating, for example, is one of those behaviors, as well as obsessively controlling them and always looking to find the slightest evidence of betrayal on their part.

You must identify these behavior patterns in yourself so that you can work on improving your attitude and keeping paranoia from affecting your relationship and taking over your life. The way you perceive yourself, your partner, your relationship, and the rest of the world can change, but this alteration must come from within and from your will. A person with these problems will never admit them when confronted. The desire for change must come from them, and it is they who must do the most work in this regard.

Since the central theme here is related to personal insecurities, it is, of course, natural that you start working on yourself, not only in your relationship with your partner but also in your relationship with yourself. It is crucial that you realize your worth and actively work to appreciate yourself for who you are and what you can achieve. Learn to love yourself and value the wonderful qualities that others see in you, including your romantic partner. Once you can see and believe what they see in you, you will stop comparing yourself to others and your inferiority complex will disappear.

Build confidence by exercising your self-esteem the old-fashioned way in front of the mirror. It may sound cliché, but starting your day with a positive message to yourself can do wonders; surround yourself with positive people and positive energy. Progress is achieved with dedication, application, and openness to change and improve your life, so a positive attitude is essential.

Visible confidence is just as important as inner confidence, so don't neglect your exterior while you work on the inside. Of course, it's the inner beauty that counts, but, indeed, our appearance can sometimes be a source of insecurity for all of us. Therefore, you need to practice loving yourself inside and out. Whether it's repeating positive messages in the mirror, coming to terms with your physical flaws, or buying a flattering piece of clothing that makes you feel amazing, taking care of your appearance will have a visible effect, in more ways than one.

This is where your partner should also help: peace of mind on your part is essential to the process. The two must work together to help you realize and believe in your worth and increase your self-esteem. They can do this by making you feel loved and appreciated. Spending quality time together and having fun is invaluable and will go a long way in solving your problems.

CHAPTER - 14
HOW TO TELL IF YOU OR YOUR PARTNER ARE JEALOUS

A crucial area in learning how to improve your relationship is understanding your existing relationship. It's impossible to know what to improve in your relationship if you don't know the weaknesses and areas for improvement. Different types of relationships require different strategies to improve, so identifying your relationship type is crucial to improving it all together. By learning the following topics, you will be able to better understand where your relationship falls and address the strategies provided in this book to help you improve it.

Understanding Emotions in Relationships

We all know that it is important to process and understand your partner's emotions. However, we often forget that we must also take into account our emotions. Most of us are so used to paying attention to other people's feelings that we don't know how to listen to our emotions. When you build an understanding of what your needs are in a relationship, you can better understand what your relationship needs in general.

Listening to Your Feelings

Knowing how to listen to your feelings is important to having a healthy relationship. For many people, this is a challenge. We live in a world where looking inward and getting in touch with the deepest parts of ourselves is not as valuable as being distracted. This is largely due to the media and consumerism, where we are constantly bombarded with information, so it's nice to unplug from it all. In addition, they sell us means of distraction wherever we go. Looking inward and getting in touch with your feelings will take practice, but it will get easier once you get used to it. There are different ways to do this, and I'll describe one of them here for you.

Commit to Doing It

The first step in listening to your feelings is committing to do so. If you are not engaged, it will be difficult for you to examine yourself without a barrier there. Once you begin to listen to your feelings, you can take steps to improve the points that make you feel negative emotions, and the first step in doing this is realizing what those emotions are.

Notice the Sensations in Your Body

Once you've committed to looking deep within yourself, you're ready to start. The best place to start is to notice when something inside you feels different. When we feel emotions, we often feel them manifesting somewhere in our bodies. Noticing tightness in your chest or a sinking feeling in your stomach is usually an indication that you are experiencing some kind of emotion. Even if you're not sure what the emotion is, noticing the cues within your body that indicate when you feel emotion is a great first step. Many people will feel an emotion and act aggressively through physical aggression or angry words and never look inward to explore the feeling or what triggered it. Take a second now to notice how your body feels inside and notice any places of tension or uneasy feelings within your body. You may be feeling some emotions right now. Bring to your awareness the changes that occur within your body when you experience an emotion so that the next time you feel it, you notice it instead of pushing it away.

Give Feelings a Name

The next step in listening to your emotions after realizing you are feeling something is to give that sensation a name. We are all aware of issues such as fear, anger, happiness, surprise, and sadness. These emotions are a good place to start.

Go Deeper

As we become adults, our emotions become more complex than those listed above. We are capable of experiencing deeper and more complicated emotions such as shame, anxiety, despair, shock, doubt, ambiguity, etc. Once you feel comfortable noticing and merely naming your emotions, try looking at them a little deeper and find out if the emotion you thought was sadness is more disappointment, for example. If you're not sure what some of these more complex emotions might be, you can name the emotion in the simplest sense (sadness, for example) and then take this word to an online thesaurus or emotion chart to see what other emotions could be related to that and thus better describe what you are feeling.

Giving yourself a larger vocabulary of emotions will help you express yourself more deeply so that you can develop a deeper understanding of yourself, and others can also develop a deeper understanding of you. Naming the emotions, you feel when the notes will allow you to express these feelings to others in the form of non-violent communication when the time comes.

Listen to Your Partner's Feelings

Once you become comfortable noticing your feelings, giving them names, and then going deeper into your exploration of them, you will be able to more easily observe and understand the feelings of others. If you can't understand your emotions, it will be quite difficult to understand your partner's reactions, even if you put them into words. Once you have some understanding of the feelings you're experiencing, you'll be able to relate to someone when they tell you they're feeling anxious, for example, as you may have felt this emotion or something similar while exploring your sentiments.

The other benefit of understanding your own emotions on a deeper level is that if your partner tells you they are feeling sad, you can deepen your understanding of reactions by combining this information with your knowledge of nonverbal communication (such as body language or facial expressions) to determine that they may be feeling something more complex. You can look at their body language, facial expressions, and things they've been saying to you in conversation, combined with being told they're feeling sad to determine if they may be feeling down or depressed. By understanding ourselves, we gain a deeper understanding of humans in general and other people with whom we interact.

Accept Yourself and Your Partner

In addition to understanding your own emotions and your partner's, a big part of having a healthy relationship is being able to accept yourself for who you are and your partner for who they are. Learning to accept yourself is part of improving your self-esteem. People with low self-esteem often have a hard time practicing self-acceptance and often end up in unhealthy relationships. Let's learn a little more about how you can use self-acceptance to improve your self-esteem so that you can function in your relationship in a healthier way.

Self-acceptance can be defined in three different ways:

1. Self-acceptance is the feeling of being satisfied with yourself despite your past choices or behaviors.
2. Self-acceptance is being aware of your strengths and weaknesses.
3. Self-acceptance is having a realistic assessment of your abilities, talents, and overall worth.

Summarizing those three definitions, self-acceptance is the happiness and satisfaction you have with yourself that is needed to achieve good self-esteem. Having self-acceptance means that you can understand who you are, be realistic about it, and be aware of the strengths and weaknesses that you have. Those who have high levels of self-acceptance tend to also have a more positive attitude, they don't want to be different from who they are, they accept all their traits of themselves, and they don't get confused with their identity.

Self-esteem is defined as having confidence in your ability, and self-acceptance is being aware of and satisfied with all your strengths and weaknesses. Self-acceptance does not need to depend on achievement for one to feel worthy. It makes people feel worthwhile simply for being comfortable and happy with who they are. When you feel comfortable with who you are, you are better able to handle conflicts and face adversity when you are in a relationship. People with low self-esteem often sacrifice their needs and happiness to care for their partner, leading to relationship toxicity and codependency.

How does self-acceptance work in the real world? Based on scientific studies, self-acceptance has five different stages. The first stage is Aversion. People's natural response to uncomfortable feelings or situations is avoidance or resistance. For example, if someone doesn't like one of his or her traits, it's natural for them to avoid them rather than confront them head-on. The second stage is Curiosity. When the aversion is no longer working, people will be curious to learn more about their problems. This curiosity is the driving factor behind people seeking to learn more about their problems. The more curious a person is, the more likely they are to have a fulfilling life.

People who lack this curiosity tend to shy away from problems and get stuck in stage one, which is aversion. The third stage is Tolerance. Those in this stage will wish their problems would go away as they put up with them all the time. Many people in this stage are still experiencing the effects of their problems, but they force themselves to tolerate them to continue with their daily lives. The fourth stage is allowing. As people's resistance slowly wears off, they allow themselves to feel. Instead of just acknowledging and tolerating, they acknowledge and feel the emotions that occur. This is the acceptance stage, where you accept your problem and allow yourself to feel all the emotions that come along with it. The fifth and final stage is Friendship. During this, people begin to see their feelings' value and decide to accept them instead of wanting them to go away. They are comfortable enough to be friends with those feelings, no matter if they are good or bad.

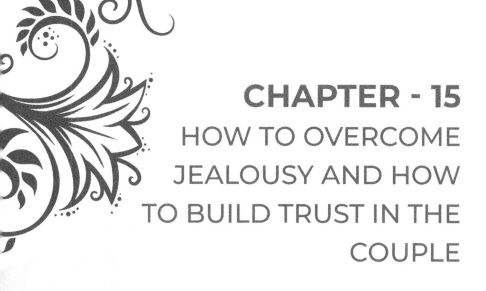

CHAPTER - 15
HOW TO OVERCOME JEALOUSY AND HOW TO BUILD TRUST IN THE COUPLE

The first step to overcoming jealousy is accepting that it exists in the first place. Not surprisingly, many people can't even admit that they have feelings of jealousy. They can't even admit it to themselves, which is a problem. You know the signs you experience, the anger and discomfort you feel whenever you feel your relationship is threatened. You know you have these seemingly exhausting feelings of jealousy, so you need to confront these emotions.

Factors to Accept About Jealousy

Accepting that you are jealous is a fact. You must also accept other facts before you can start working on your jealousy.

1. **Jealousy won't go away overnight:** Don't make the false assumption that your feelings of jealousy will suddenly vanish into thin air. Recognize that jealousy is present and that you need to learn to deal with it without allowing it to take over your beautiful life and relationship. This is a feeling that has probably resulted from an underlying problem with your confidence or self-assurance. Realize

that it may take you some time to learn to deal with this feeling. You may have to do a lot of work on yourself before you finally start to feel in control of your emotions again.

2. **You have to confide in your partner about your jealousy:** Remember that the object of your jealousy is your partner, and they probably don't feel comfortable with the signs of jealousy they see in you. They may have even tried to make sure you have it all to yourself but it still doesn't lessen these feelings of jealousy. So why not talk to them about your feelings instead of expressing anger or frustration or blaming them for something that might be on your mind? Remember that you love this person. So have that conversation with them where you refrain from blaming them, but try to be as open as possible. You can say something like, "I get these jealous feelings every time I see you chatting with... I know I shouldn't feel this way, but I can't seem to help it. I would love for you to help me deal with these feelings." An understanding partner should be able to treat the problem as another challenge facing the relationship and not let their partner figure things out on their own. You and your partner must now accept that there is a jealousy issue that needs to be resolved. Hopefully, with the full support of your partner, you can begin to take positive steps to work through jealousy.

3. **Make room for jealousy:** Hard as it may seem, we all need to make room for jealousy in our lives, especially in love relationships. We need to realize that life itself is complex, as are relationships. We only want to experience good times, but we are forced to realize that we are facing bad times. Your beloved partner will sometimes annoy you, frustrate you and even drive you crazy. Nobody gets rid

of their partner because they made them angry. You could probably do that to someone else who means absolutely nothing to you—like a random stranger on a train who stole your seat. But when it comes to someone you love and are probably engaged to, you have to learn to deal with their emotions, which, unfortunately, can include some jealousy at times.

4. **_Some things are just out of your control:_** People are made differently, as are their attitudes towards life and other people in general. Some people are very outgoing and "extra friendly," while others are introverted and more reserved. Imagine that your partner was a very outgoing guy, and that's how you met them in the first place. Suddenly, you realize that you start to feed feelings of jealousy and get angry at how they relate so freely to others. You insist that they need to change their ways for you, forgetting that this is how you met, accepted, and fell in love with this person in the first place. It is not your partner's fault that he or she is probably very attractive or very gifted and therefore naturally attracts a lot of attention. How could you control that? Other factors are also out of anyone's control, like your partner's job. This may mean that they interact with many people who, to you, may seem like threats. What about people whose partners are actors or politicians or those in the media and sports? Face it—you just can't control everything. It's best to focus on learning to control yourself and taking positive steps to get rid of jealousy.

5. **_Accept yourself:_** I'm sure you've heard a thousand and one motivational speeches about self-confidence and believing in yourself. It's not that easy, right? How about you realize that was the reason for your jealousy? Would you start to

appreciate yourself a little more? You must understand that you are unique as you are and the truth of this statement depends on your way of thinking. Do you think you're smart? Handsome? Talented? Do you realize that there may be someone out there who possesses more of these qualities than you? But does that stop you from believing that you are all these things and more? No, it shouldn't! If your partner chose you, then there must be some unique quality in you that he or she saw and desired. Enough of telling yourself that you may not be good enough for your partner or that someone else might be a better fit than you. Stop telling yourself that you don't look as good as when you met your partner. Enough of those other false beliefs that you conjured up in your mind over time. It's okay to take some positive steps to boost your confidence. For example, getting a new job, going back to school, living a healthier lifestyle, or making wardrobe changes. But these changes will not prevent your jealousy; first of all, you do not believe in yourself and appreciate yourself for the unique individual that you are.

We now understand the different reasons why jealousy can occur in a relationship, and acceptance is key to addressing jealousy and dealing with it in general. Now we will see more practical ways to overcome these feelings that have been invading your mind and your relationship.

Step 1: First, Identify the Cause of Your Jealousy

Jealousy doesn't work like that on a person, and by now you need to understand that your partner may be the object of your jealousy, not the reason. Something they do or say may trigger your jealousy, but you can't blame them for these feelings if you want to get over the jealousy. The reason for your jealousy has to do with you fundamentally, and it is time to determine the cause. I have put together some important questions that you can answer. Hopefully, your honest answers will lead you to identify the exact cause of your feelings of jealousy towards your partner. These questions have been divided into different categories based on what I have found to be the main causes of jealousy.

Step 2: Acknowledge Your Jealousy

If you've been able to identify what's causing your jealousy (i.e., insecurities, low self-esteem, fear, or self-doubt), then that's great! Now we can move on to the next step of overcoming jealousy. If you're still unsure where the jealousy stems from, hopefully, you've got it right after this stage. Then you can properly learn to deal with these feelings. Here we will see how to recognize your jealousy in an efficient and viable way—through writing.

Over the years, psychology experts have used this method of writing about feelings like anger, worry, hurt, and unforgiveness to help people confront their thoughts and emotions so they can deal with them appropriately. It is also a way to positively motivate yourself and feed your mind with the kind of feelings you want to have or the kind of person you want to be. For example, a person who thinks she is not pretty can write somewhere conspicuous a positive way he or she would see herself.

Writing affirmations like "I am beautiful inside and out," "I am an attractive man/woman," and "I am a unique person" and reading them to yourself every day can help you gradually increase your low self-esteem and become more confident. This approach can also work for jealousy if you can write honestly about your feelings. It will reveal to you to what extent your jealousy is affecting your relationship. Get a notepad and paper (or whatever works for you) and get started.

Step 3: Turn Your Jealousy Into Pride

"Jealousy is not you, and you are not jealousy," says Robert Leahy in the book "The Jealousy Cure." He also explains that you can see jealousy as a breath of air, that we inhale and exhale without even paying attention to it. This means that jealousy can be something that goes in and out of our minds. The problem arises when jealousy stays in our thoughts and begins to take control. Jealousy should be viewed as an emotion that can come and go like anger or hurt. You can't keep feeling angry all the time, can you? It eventually wears off, as does the jealousy.

Let's see how to channel jealousy into a more positive feeling like pride. Pride in this sense means that instead of feeling all the anger and resentment towards your partner, you start to see the good in them and are proud of them and your relationship. Pride here also means countering your jealous thoughts with more energy and positive feelings.

For example, in the case of Lenny and his partner, instead of thinking, "Lenny could be cheating on me with that man," counter those thoughts with prideful thoughts like "I love and trust my partner, I'm sure she's just chatting with him." "A coworker she met at the party," or "Lenny wouldn't stoop so low as to cheat on me, she's very outgoing and friendly, and I like that about her." It may not be that easy to chase away the jealous thought. If you get in the habit of turning jealous thoughts into proud, positive thoughts and counteracting your jealousy, these feelings will start to creep in. Now you can truly focus on your relationship.

Here are some more tips on how to turn jealousy into pride:

1. **Fill your mind with reasons why you should be proud of your relationship:** As we said, jealous thoughts can come and go, and you can be in control of your headspace. Try to fill your mind with reasons you should be proud of your partner instead of jealous whenever these thoughts come up. If it bothers you so much, then write down the reasons. "I am proud of Lenny because she is smart and makes me very happy," "I am proud of Lenny because she is someone I can count on to be there for me all the time," "She has always been true to me," "She makes many sacrifices because of our relationship," "She is great with my family." If you get into the habit of reminding yourself of the proud and positive traits that have kept you in love, I bet your jealousy will start to fade.

2. **Have self-confidence all the time:** Enough can never be said about how a lack or low self-confidence leads to jealousy. So, get confident. Believe that you are enough for your partner and that he or she understands you. Remember the great characteristics you possess and why your partner is lucky to be with you. If you don't play your trumpet, who will? Tell yourself, "I am handsome/beautiful, funny, hard-working, and a great partner." Just put love on yourself! If it helps, then write down these positive statements to remind yourself and tell yourself whenever you find yourself caught up in jealous thoughts. Invest in reading motivational books that can boost your confidence if you find them helpful. Jealousy is unlikely to stay on your mind for long if you have confidence in yourself.

3. **Stop comparing yourself to others:** Remember that everyone is unique in their way, so stop comparing yourself to that guy or woman your partner might be chatting with. Nobody

can be you, so believe in yourself. Comparisons can create envy and jealousy. No need to say it again—be proud of yourself. When the jealous thoughts start, and you think, "It's because I don't drive the kind of car he drives," "I'm not as pretty as her." Counter those thoughts with, "His car is great, and mine is good enough for me now, I worked hard for it." "I am an intelligent and attractive woman."

4. **Believe in your partner:** Have some faith in the partner you have chosen. Believe in them and decide to trust and be proud of them all the time. Let your partner know that you are pleased and trust them, even though you can see the threats around you. It helps them to respect you and be proud of you as well for the level of maturity and confidence that you are showing instead of jealousy.

5. **Meditate on the positive and not on the negative:** Try to focus on positive thoughts instead of negative fictions and imaginations as a result of jealousy. Keep your imagination positive about your partner by all means. Instead of thinking, "They're staying up late because they're with someone else," which is a negative thought, replace that belief with a proud one like, "My partner is mature and thinks highly of me; He probably has a good reason why he's late tonight."

6. **Be grateful:** Develop the habit of being grateful for what you have in your life. Thank your partner and the joy they bring you. When the jealousy returns, remind yourself what you are grateful for and feel proud and thankful.

Step 4: Ignore the Competition

"They're not your competition if you don't even compete," says an anonymous writer. There is no open competition except the one we create. Much of the jealousy derives fundamentally from comparing or relating to others. We think, "Why is that guy always trying to talk to my partner? Does he think he's better than me?" "He has a better job than me. Maybe that's what she sees in him," "Maybe if I were as thin as her, he would pay more attention to me." Many of these thoughts go through our heads and create feelings of jealousy. But, why the comparison?

There is a fundamental part of our primitive nature that wants to compete. This is like the animals we see in the jungle that compete for almost everything, including food, territory, and mates. But we are not the animals of the jungle, and we have higher and more advanced capacities to control some of these instincts. We are unique in ourselves and instead of comparing ourselves and letting jealousy take a better part of us, we can focus on our relationships and ourselves. We can continue to add value to ourselves and do what we want to do, not because of the influence of any competition.

Step 5: Handle Awkward Situations Like a Pro

People wonder how to handle awkward situations with their partners without getting jealous. For example, how do you handle other men talking to your female partner when you are there watching and probably waiting? How do you handle others dancing with your partner? Giving them hugs, maybe kisses? Does that arouse jealousy in you? Some of these situations can be overwhelming, almost like a temptation asking you to get upset or fight with your partner. But there is always the right way to handle things without exploding into a fit of jealousy and wreaking havoc on your relationship.

CHAPTER - 16
UNDERSTANDING THE PHASES OF RELATIONSHIPS

I f you are in a relationship that seems to be headed toward commitment, such as getting engaged, getting married, having children, etc., it may be a good idea to get acquainted with life. There are five stages to all relationships. Pairs move through the various stages at different speeds and will move back and forth from stage to stage and sometimes find themselves in the same stage and other times in a different state. Understanding the stages helps the couple normalize what they are experiencing and make better decisions.

1. **Romantic stage:** All relationships begin with this stage. The need met here is love and belonging. This stage is characterized by your dream as dualities, fantasies, and hopes for the future. The role of this stage is to give the couple a taste of the potential of their union. This stage lasts between 2 months and 2 years but has an average of 6 months. When a person is in this stage, his or her body produces large amounts of endorphins, which makes them feel unusually happy, positive, and excited about everything in their lives. There is not much to fix, and

couples are encouraged to continue exploring each other.

2. **Struggle for power stage:** During the exploration process, differences are discovered and a power struggle ensues. This is the most difficult of all the stages and is usually the time when relationships end. As couples become emotionally and physically more intimate, weaknesses and vulnerabilities begin to surface and conflicts arise.

The satisfied need now is power and some freedom. The role of this stage is to make each individual aware of himself and his partner and begin to relate to each other as a whole person. The power struggle begins shortly after the two move together and can last for many bitter years. During this stage, a couple has three options: break up, stay together but live parallel lives, or learn to fight fairly both by winning and declaring individuality.

3. **Stability stage:** If we did not learn coping skills as a child, then the power struggle phase was exceptionally difficult. However, by surviving, the couple comes to terms with each other's differences and establishes clear boundaries. The need satisfied at this stage is freedom and choice.

The danger at this stage is that the couple may begin to realize that each other's life paths may be different. There is a sense of loss and sadness as dreams do not materialize. There may be a feeling of boredom, a feeling of not being connected and having nothing in common. The focus is on the present, not the future because that is not decided yet.

This is the second most common stage for counseling or divorce. At first, it feels good to agree to stop changing the other, but life is about growth and change. At this stage, the couple has history and must use it as an advantage to persevere in the relationship. Mutual respect is established or the couple reverts to a power struggle.

4. **Commitment stage:** This is the stage where the couple should consider marriage; unfortunately, people are usually already married in the romantic stage. That's unfortunate because when they get to the power struggle stage, they wonder what hit them. In this stage, the couple is making clear decisions about themselves and their partner, based on both differences and commonalities.

The needs met here are a balance of love, belonging, fun, power, and freedom. This is a stage where two people realize they don't need to be together but choose to be. Generally, this is the stage where the couple finally begins to feel comfortable and happy with their deepening relationship. Some people feel a sense of loss at this stage as they learn to accept their partner for who they are, as this means they have to let go of the fantasy of who they want their partner to be. In this phase, people begin to reestablish their outside interests and friendships, which were abandoned in the romantic phase. There is some danger that the couple may begin to distance themselves or become bored with each other. The remedy is to try to maintain the connection that was created in the romance phase by setting up a date night, flirting, and making each other a priority.

5. **Co-creation stage:** At this stage, the couple has decided to be a team that moves to the world. This may include children, a project, a joint business venture, etc. The role of this stage is to handle any common project or life crisis as a perfect team, acting as one: proactive, responsible, and constructive for mutual fulfillment. The danger at this stage

is that relations with the outside world are neglected. The relationship must be continually nurtured along the way. There has to be time for you, for me, for us, and them. This is difficult at times and decisions must be made.

CHAPTER - 17
WHY ARE THERE COUPLE CONFLICTS?

To face the monster in your relationship and face your fears, the first step is to understand the source of the conflict between you and your partner and resolve it appropriately.

You won't be able to fully adjust the tensions in your relationship if you don't put your finger on the exact source of the problem. To effectively solve a problem, you need to know its roots. Otherwise, all you can do is put a Band-Aid on the problem. Small tensions can spark big fights when issues remain unresolved.

The first thing you need to do to overcome conflicts in your relationship is to identify and acknowledge them.

As I mentioned in my introduction, there are many reasons for the situation your relationship is going through today. I will review some of these reasons.

Conflicts Caused by Professional Life

Tensions may arise because you care more about your career than your partner, or at least one of you may think so. This situation can cause your partner or yourself to react strongly. There is nothing worse than feeling abandoned by someone you love.

Focusing more on your professional life than your personal life is not only unhealthy when you're single, it's detrimental when you're in a relationship.

Sometimes it's really hard to reconcile work and family, especially when you want to start a business or have a very stressful job. But, to have a balanced life and avoid conflicts in your relationship, it is essential to learn to disconnect from work and enjoy life with your loved ones.

Infidelity and Inappropriate Behavior

There are attitudes to prohibit when you are in a relationship. If you stick to behavior that your partner finds unforgivable, you'll have trouble picking up the pieces and your relationship will inevitably experience periods of turbulence.

There may also be conflicts between couples in the case of infidelity. If you find yourself in this situation, you will face struggles that are beyond the scope of this book. Seek therapy, either for yourself or for both of you.

When Your Partner No Longer Meets Your Expectations

Life evolves, grows, and changes. Relationships do too. Sometimes two people in a relationship grow apart and reach a point where they are no longer the people they were when they started the relationship.

When this happens, sit down and have a conversation about it. What expectations do any of you have that are not being met? Are these expectations reasonable? The only way to measure the state of the relationship is to talk about it.

To overcome conflicts in your love life, whatever the source of the tensions, the first point you should try to understand is why the conflicts are there in the first place. To do this, talk to your partner. The discussion can be uncomfortable, but it is necessary. Your anxiety may increase, but don't let it force you into rash behavior. Calm discussions do more for conflict than anxiety-fueled discussions.

Many couples try to avoid fighting as much as possible. Others will blame the other person for being the cause of the arguments. These reactions do not resolve the struggles and can even exacerbate the problems.

Fights are an ordinary part of life and relationships. When ignored, they deal more damage. When confronted head-on, they become tools to help couples grow closer when resolving conflicts together.

Fights can arise from wrong assumptions about:

- The nature of the relationship.
- Various assumptions about how things should be done in the house.
- Works.
- The various obligations of each partner.
- Contrasts in morals, values, needs, or desires.
- Bad communication.

What Conflicts Do to Anxiety

When problems arise in a relationship, you may feel that all your anxieties are justified and ultimately turn out to be true. Don't give in to this way of thinking! Anxiety stems from the unknown, and conflicts arise when expectations are not met or differences of opinion are brought to light. They are healthy when handled properly, while anxiety is nothing but detrimental. Some of the ways that conflict can affect anxiety include:

Increase in Cardiac Frequency

Conflict can cause a release of adrenaline, which anxiety only makes worse. This can lead to a rapid heartbeat which, in turn, leads to shortness of breath and increased anxiety thanks to these physiological symptoms. It is a vicious circle. The best way to combat this is to approach the conflict calmly. If you avoid raising your voice, getting angry, or reacting in anger, you will not trigger an adrenaline release and therefore calm anxious feelings.

Nervous Energy or Movement

Again, thanks to the adrenaline, your whole body will react by suddenly filling up with energy that has to be used in some way. Since during an argument you most likely won't be running or fighting, that energy translates into pacing, toe-tapping, hand wringing, and general fidgeting and energetic tics. These can be uncomfortable for you and distract your partner when you are in the middle of a conflict. Of course, it's not your fault, but that knowledge doesn't make it go away. As stated above, approach the situation calmly rather than anxiously to avoid the release of adrenaline.

Panic and Anxiety Attacks

Can anxiety lead to anxiety attacks?
This may not be new information, but it's good for your health to remember that in conflict, it's in your best interest to stay calm if you're struggling with anxiety and panic. The situation can trigger an attack, which can make everything worse. Panic and anxiety attacks are typically characterized by:

- Difficulty breathing.
- Difficulty focusing.

- Sweating.
- Racing thoughts.
- Feeling of impending doom.

Needless to say, these are not fun symptoms, and it's worth keeping in mind before you get into an argument that if you don't stay level-headed, it could lead to a seizure.

Defensive Behavior

Nothing is more detrimental to constructive conflict resolution than defensiveness. Anxiety can block the more rational part of your mind from thinking through a situation logically. Without this logic, you may find it difficult to focus on what your partner is saying and instead of listening, cause you to lash out and become defensive, even if your partner is not attacking you. While you absolutely must stand up for yourself when you're being treated unfairly, if your partner is looking for a peaceful resolution, the best course of action is to agree with their intentions and stop being defensive. Of course, when you have anxiety, that's not so easy.

Tendency to Turn Off

Instead of getting defensive, you may just shut down completely. The anxious mind may be unable to process what is happening and lack the energy to resolve the situation, leading to a complete shutdown. When this happens, you can't focus or concentrate, you can't use logic or rationality to resolve a conflict, and you may even be unable to understand what your partner is saying. Inside, you will feel heavy and empty, like a battery that suddenly died. The best thing to do when this happens is to rest and recover. Conflicts will remain until you can get your mind back and put your rationality in charge.

CHAPTER - 18
HOW TO RESOLVE CONFLICTS AND SAVE YOUR RELATIONSHIP

When you are faced with a conflict in your growing relationship, think about the way you express your feelings or talk about this conflict with your partner. Good communication is where everyone can take stock and try to understand each other's attitudes. Conflict will be easier to manage when it isn't exacerbated by angry tones and unnecessary insults.

For effective conflict communication, there are 3 rules to follow:

1. Avoid raising your voice and remain calm whenever a conflict occurs.
2. Allow your partner to speak and develop your argument because communication involves not only talking but also listening.
3. Look for a middle ground, but do not make concessions that may have negative consequences in the future.

A couple who argues but respects these three rules will find it easier to reach a solution.

Some actions are necessary to overcome the conflict between

couples. Relationships are not always easy and you are constantly learning. Is it possible not to repeat the same mistakes and stabilize the love relationship?

How can you handle conflict in your relationships without becoming a doormat?

Follow these recommendations to rebuild love in a difficult relationship:

- Once you understand the reasons for the tensions in your relationship, you can move on to the more "direct" phase of reconciliation. The first step can indeed be very psychological because you have to communicate with your partner.

- It is necessary to implement more technical and thoughtful actions to find the heart of your partner and overcome the crisis in your relationship.

- The actions you have decided to implement must correspond to the different issues, otherwise, the latter will have no particular effect and may even aggravate the situation.

- Don't look for a solution only to end it; look for a solution to improve it.

- Don't blame either party. Relationships are a team effort, and both must be fully involved or not at all.

- If your partner or yourself are feeling unfulfilled in your relationship, you should spend time together to better understand your problems and what you both need from the relationship.

Every relationship experiences conflict at one point or another. It is important to know that disagreement is not necessarily a bad thing, it is a way that people express their different points of view on a situation or topic.

Conflict Resolution in Healthy Relationships

Communication is the fuel that sustains a relationship. When we say that a relationship is healthy, it means that the partners value communication and never allow a lack of communication to affect their union. A good way to develop a healthy relationship is to practice successful conflict resolution without the interference of a third party.

It is normal to disagree on some issues; however, constant conflict is a sign of an unhealthy relationship. If you're arguing with your partner about trivial matters like what kind of friends you hang out with, where to go out for dinner or a night out, and who should handle what chores around the house, then these tips are for you. They will help you resolve all your arguments amicably:

- **Do not cross your limits:** treat everyone with the respect they deserve, whether you are angry or not. Don't respond in the same way if your partner ridicules you, calls you names, and uses provocative words during the argument. Instead of responding to him or her, try to remain calm and walk away if they are not giving in to your request to stop. Let them know that you can continue the discussion when tensions are lower.

- **Find out the root of the matter:** the discussion does not come out of empty space; there must be a reason for it. An effective way to resolve a conflict is to unmask the real problem. Try to understand your partner. Maybe they need special attention or just feel insecure. Knowing the root cause of an argument will help you resolve it amicably. The summary of the point I'm trying to make here is that you shouldn't shy away from the real problem.

- **Always resolve conflicts:** It is always in your best interest to resolve every issue that comes up. Never pretend that everything is fine while something is building inside of you. Your goal is to have a healthy relationship; everything needs to be out in the open. Indeed, they cannot always be on the same page, but they must respect each other's differences.

- **Compromise when necessary:** Commitment is one of the ingredients of a healthy relationship. You don't have to be determined to win the argument every time. You just have to let go of some situations and accept that you are wrong.

- **Take note of everything:** You should not be indifferent to your partner. You need to take the time to consider the things that are bothering them and also consider whether you are taking advantage of them or being considerate enough. From what angle does your partner see problems? You need to find answers to these and many more questions as they will help you understand your partner better.

If you've tried all of the above tricks and the arguments persist, you should now look in the compatibility area. Are you compatible with each other? If the answer is yes, then learn to work together and implement everything you have learned from this book.

Conflict is a way of expressing our differences, but it should not degenerate into physical attacks or rain of abuse on each other. This is never acceptable and is the opposite of a healthy relationship. Never allow verbal abuse by either party and know when to end an argument if you find it is going in that direction. Keep in your mind the knowledge that one of the signs of an unhealthy relationship is when one partner has a dominant attitude and when one partner tries to manipulate or control the other at all times.

Finally, pay attention to what annoys your partner. Here are some of the situations that can upset your partner:

- You're always making excuses to avoid doing things with them (and you may wonder why you do it).
- Instead of spending time with your partner, you go out with friends (do you spend the same amount of time with your partner and your friends?).
- You don't pay attention to them when they speak.
- You don't answer your text or call after a reasonable period.

How to Resolve Conflicts in Your Relationships in Advance

Successfully overcoming conflict in a relationship is a good thing, and everything may seem rosy for a while. Of course, another problem will arise, but you must not allow these crises to recur too often because constant conflict can lead to long-term separation. Disputes can take on a life of their own and turn into arguments that threaten the relationship.

Therefore, you must be prepared to anticipate these problems and do what you can to make your partner (and yourself) happy, not only during crises but also in everyday life. To do this, give everything in the relationship without waiting for the tensions to start. Don't wait for arguments, anticipate them and work to resolve them before they break out, and you'll see that your partner will act in the same way.

CHAPTER - 19
HOW TO HELP YOUR PARTNER WITH RELATIONSHIP ANXIETY

One of the most important things that the spouse of an anxious person has to recognize is that the partner's role in the process is one of support. It may be the case that you know your partner better than anyone else, but that still leaves the task of dealing with anxiety mostly up to them and not you. This doesn't mean that you should let anxiety symptoms eat away at the person until they irreparably damage their life, but it means that your place in the bigger picture needs to be recognized by you and your companion.

The role of the supporter is important. Sure, sitting on the sidelines can be frustrating at times, but solid support is just what your partner needs right now. Also, if you're the one dealing with anxiety, these tips will help you understand the kinds of things your spouse can do for you.

1. ***Understand that overcoming anxiety is a process (anxiety is not something someone can quickly get out of).*** Anxiety is not like having a common cold. It's not something you get and experience a finger-snap resolution of. Anxiety disorders should be considered conditions that require

treatment. What this means for the partner of an anxious person is that you need to be realistic about your partner's anxiety. They won't get out of their anxiety, and it's more than a little unfair of you to expect them to. As a supporter of an anxious person, it is critical to recognize that you will help them through the long process of overcoming their illness.

2. **Be aware of your dysfunctional thoughts or preconceived notions.** Anxiety is characterized by a cavalcade of dysfunctional thoughts that people are often unaware they are having. Unfortunately for significant others of anxious people, they may have a spiral of dysfunctional thoughts that can affect how they perceive and interact with their anxious partner. The meaning here is not that the couple is necessarily at risk of concern, but simply that they need to recognize how their interaction with their partner may be affected by notions about their condition (including the subconscious stigma that men and women often have towards mind conditions).

3. **Make sure things are going to work out.** One of the most important things someone supporting another person through anxiety (or any condition) can do is reassure them that things are going to be okay. This does not mean telling a lie. If someone has a terminal illness like stage IV cancer, it's important to recognize exactly what that means. But honest reassurance in the case of anxiety is a bit different. Anxiety can and often does get better, so reminding your partner of this can put a positive thought in their head that can be an important part of creating real change in their life.

4. **Encourage your partner to seek help.** The hard reality for

some couples of anxious people to accept is that it's not their job to guide their partner in the direction they think they should go. We have established that anxiety disorders are conditions that generally do not improve without treatment, but that does not mean that it is your role as their support to force them into treatment or to dictate what form treatment should take.

Intervention-type maneuvers can be problematic in mental health. This is especially true in the case of anxiety, where the individual may already be inclined to have a suspicious or fearful approach to others or the world in general. Forcing or cornering your partner into treatment is not a good idea for anxious people. What you can do is find out what help is available for their condition and encourage them to seek help. That's all you can do.

5. **Be patient while your partner overcomes his condition.** It's important to be patient when dealing with a person who has a mental health condition and this is as true for anxiety as it is for other conditions like depression. Let us remember that anxiety disorders include conditions as divergent as GAD, specific phobias, and obsessive-compulsive disorder. The point here is that some of these conditions can be very debilitating for the individual treating them and very frustrating for the partner or family member around them. For your sanity (and for your partner's sake), it's important to be patient. The change will happen slowly and it will help you to keep this in mind.

6. **Provide ongoing education and support for your partner.** Being supportive means being someone your partner can turn to when they need help. Again, the goal here is not to force your partner to do something they may not be

ready for but to support them when they decide to make a change and to take steps to bring about that change. As a support partner, you can provide ongoing education about anxiety and related conditions, such as depression, and you can even find ways to pass this information on to your partner.

Anxious people can have excessive or unnecessary overreactions to stimuli, so you and your partner need to recognize that you're playing a supportive role. If your companion feels that you are trying to manipulate or push them in a particular direction, they may start to distrust you and avoid you. Therefore, you must address your partner's anxious symptoms from the point of view of educating you and them on this topic.

7. ***Recognize that no one understands your partner's anxiety more than your partner.*** No matter how much you educate yourself about anxiety, no one is better equipped to understand your partner's anxiety than them. Sure, you may be around them for several hours of the day, and you may feel like you can see aspects of their anxiety that they may seem unaware of, but since you're not experiencing what they are and you're not inside their head to know the triggers, you may not understand their condition as well as you might think. Use this as an opportunity for your partner to educate you about their concerns, not the other way around.

8. ***Be available, not bossy.*** It's easy to fall into the trap of being bossy when you're in a relationship and you notice that your partner needs help with something. You may find that you have an inordinate desire to help them, and you may feel that you can see matters from a vantage point

that they may not. Even if that is the case, your partner has the ability and the right to make decisions for themselves. Loved one or not, you do not necessarily have the right to force him to do what you want him to do if he is not a danger to himself or others. If you are interested in maintaining a loving relationship with your partner, you need to focus on being available when supportive instead of being bossy.

9. **Take your partner's comments seriously.** One of the ways you learn the nature of your partner's anxiety (and get a deeper sense of what's going on) is by talking to them. Your partner's anxiety is just that, their anxiety, and you should let them give you clues as to how they feel and why. Therefore, it is important to talk to your partner and practice active listening as a support partner. Just as your anxious partner may hang on to your every word, you must learn to pay attention to your partner's words. When your partner tells you something about themselves or what's going on, take it seriously.

10. **Remember that empathy is important.** Sympathy is a word that many people understand, although they do not always show it. It involves feeling compassion and tolerance for others, a feeling that comes from a deep understanding of where the other person comes from. We can show sympathy for others through our words, actions, or even facial expressions. However, empathy is something different. Empathy involves sharing the feelings of others: actually, experiencing what they are experiencing. Although having true empathy for someone with a mental condition can be fraught with danger, this is something many couples can do and their relationships can improve

through it.

Having empathy for your partner means that you recognize that their anxiety is not just an illness they are dealing with, but may somehow be a part of it. They may have dealt with anxiety in one way or another for most of their life and may not understand how to live without their anxious, obsessive, or compulsive behaviors. By truly getting to experience the world the way they do, you can be a true supporter: someone who can deal with their ups and downs along with them.

CHAPTER - 20
THE MOST POPULAR AND DANGEROUS MISTAKES ANXIOUS PEOPLE MAKE

Maintaining a stable relationship with an anxious person is very difficult. Anxiety tends to affect every aspect of your life, including your love life. It takes most of your time as you spend it thinking about yourself instead of your lover. People can make some of these mistakes in a relationship if overwhelmed by anxiety.

They Lack Time for Their Partners

People with anxiety do not have time for their lovers since they spend most of their time thinking about their worries. This often results in procrastination, so they put off problems in their relationship for another day. People who procrastinate in their relationships find that they must stay in the relationship and end their affairs.

Not having time for your partners will result in stress, lack of confidence, and low self-esteem. If someone ignores their partner, the partner will feel unloved, neglected, and less important. This will stress them out and lower their self-esteem. They will lose trust in their partners and will resent it. They will also feel discouraged and will eventually end their relationship.

A relationship in which the partners do not have time for each other will develop at a low rate. They will spend more time complaining about problems in their relationship. There will be no peace in that relationship, so you will not be able to get together and discuss how to improve.

They Doubt Their Partner's Love

Anxious people do not believe that their partners like them. They feel anxious about whether they remain attractive to their partners, whether their partners cheat on them, whether their partners have the same future goals as theirs, or whether they have different core values.

Anxious people always worry about their physical appearance. They keep wondering if they are still attractive enough to impress their lovers. This brings insecurity as they will think that other people are more attractive to their partners. They will feel insecure, thinking that these attractive people will take away their lovers. They will go ahead and look for other ways to enhance their beauty. These acts will end up annoying their lovers, so they will end up disappointed and blaming themselves.

Anxious people worry that their partners will cheat on them. They continue to broach the subject of dishonesty in their relationships. This can annoy the companion, who may decide to end the affair. This anxiety stresses them out and they may decide to take actions that negatively affect their lives. Some commit suicide when their lovers leave, never to return.

They will doubt if their partners have the same future goals or not. For example, a woman may be planning to marry her man in the next two years, but she is not sure that her man is ready to marry her. She becomes anxious about it. This will cause other problems such as stress, anger, lack of trust, avoidance, and suspicion.

They Get Stressed Over Little Things

Anxious people are often stressed by small mistakes made by their lovers. They are mostly affected by time. When they have scheduled their time to meet, and their lovers do not meet the time, they get stressed. They make judgments that adversely affect their relationships. They also feel that their partners give them less importance.

Stress in relationships makes people feel withdrawn. When they retire, they will not have time for their partners. They will avoid meeting with their partners, which will lead to suspicion and eventually the end of the relationship. Withdrawal in a relationship discourages intimacy. Anxious people make these mistakes, which is why their relationships lack intimacy.

Anxious and stressed couples become irritable and angry. When they are angry with their partners, their partners may feel rejected and unwanted. Stress will make a person say unpleasant words to her companion. Their couple will also start to act the same way, and the relationship will go nowhere.

In addition to the situation, stress can cause frustration and pain. A stressed person may not respond to her partner during a conversation. If this is not acted upon immediately, it can widen the gap between the lovers, and the relationship can easily come to an end.

They Avoid Conversations

Anxiety interferes with the ability to communicate effectively and respond to questions. An anxious person will not have direct speech and will therefore tend to avoid conversations. A relationship will never prosper without effective communication.

If your partner does not have anxiety, it will be very difficult for you to understand what is going on in your partner's mind. If that is the case, arguments will easily arise in the relationship.

They Draw Unsubstantiated Conclusions

Anxious people jump to conclusions quickly when faced with problems in their relationships. They always draw negative conclusions about matters they are not sure about. They don't listen to their lover's explanation of why a certain thing happened. Jumping to conclusions interferes with the information the other partner is trying to deliver.

Jumping to conclusions is a behavior commonly seen in people suffering from depression as a result of anxiety. When a lover tries to comment on something, they see the comment as negative. They use phrases like "I know what you are going to say..." or "stop it..."

An example, one day Grace asked her lover to go swimming. Her lover replied that swimming was dangerous, but before she finished, Grace jumped to the conclusion. She said that her boyfriend did not support her hobby and therefore did not love her. This led to a heated argument that ultimately led to her breaking up.

People who jump to conclusions think they are always right. They do not allow their lovers to explain their perceptions. They draw negative and contrary conclusions about their lover's intentions. This leads to misunderstandings in the relationship and can eventually to a breakup.

They Don't Want to Seem Too Eager

Anxious people don't pose problems in their relationships because they don't want to seem too anxious. Being anxious means wanting something very much, especially when it is interesting or enjoyable. Enthusiasm makes someone impatient. An anxious person may be eager to love but represses this feeling of longing. Anxious people are afraid of showing their partner too much love because they don't want to appear too anxious. They worry that they will be disappointed in the end by their partners, who may not show them much love in return. This makes the partner feel unloved because they are worried about looking too anxious.

On the other hand, partners in a relationship should openly talk about their excitement without worrying about appearing too eager. Being open in a relationship greatly improves the relationship because you can talk about issues that affect both of you without fear of coming across as overly anxious.

They Overthink Everything

Anxiety makes people overthink everything. They overthink in multiple ways, including; worrying about frightening thoughts that are not likely to happen but that you constantly think about.

They Constantly Wonder When Their Relationships Will End

They begin to wonder if their relationship has any real meaning or if they are wasting their time. Even though their partners stay with them and support them during their times of anxiety, they fail to see the meaning of the relationship. They think that their partners only stay for their interests.

They also don't understand why their partners love them and not someone else. They do not appreciate their partner's efforts to show them love; if their partners are not appreciated for their love, they get disappointed and leave the relationship.

They Feel Insecure About Nothing

Anxious people begin to believe that their partners are cheating on them even though they are not. They believe that their partners will be happier with someone more normal than them, who is not anxious and causes chaos in their relationship. Sometimes they feel that they are less important to their lovers, and their partners may be interested in other people.

They Become Too Dependent on Their Partners

Anxious people become too dependent on their partners for support and security. They often worry about scary things that might happen, as their relationship might end in the future. They persistently ask their partners to assure them that they will not leave them. This can be very upsetting and can easily cause a partner to leave the relationship.

Anxious people spend most of their time worrying about other things and therefore may not have time to do their work. This heavy load will eventually find its way to its companions. Your partners will have to take responsibility for doing most of the work. It can be doing laundry, cooking, making phone calls, and shopping.

They Don't Understand the Meaning of Healthy Fights in Their Relationships

When you are anxious, it will be difficult to deal with any argument. A healthy relationship must have a healthy discussion. Anxiety will make it difficult for you to deal with your anxious thoughts when you are in a heated discussion. You will start to feel unloved, and you will never meet the right guy for you.

Your partner may ask you for something that turns into a heated argument because the anxiety makes you angry. Anger flares up at any time when triggered by things that make you anxious. For example, your partner may remind you to put enough salt in food when you cook. This can arouse your anger and you may find yourself unleashing nasty words on your spouse. This will be an argument that when you are anxious, you will find a reason to end the relationship.

They Fail to Maintain Long Distance Relationships

When their partners live far away from them, they will worry about the bad things their partners may be doing. Especially when they don't respond to calls and texts, they often think their partners are doing something fishy. They may think that their partners are cheating on them with people who are more attractive compared to them. This leads to a feeling of insecurity.

They Reject the Romantic Interests of Their Lovers

An anxious person will never accept romantic requests from their partner. They refuse to go on romantic dates, weddings, baby showers, and Christmas parties. When they think about these activities, they become stressed. All this stress is caused by anxiety and depression.

They refuse to go to public places due to low self-esteem caused by anxiety. They may be concerned about their physical appearance and what people think of them.

They Lack the Courage to Date

Anxious people are afraid of falling in love because they suffer from depression. They worry about many things like; Do I look attractive to be loved by a person of the opposite sex? Am I capable of maintaining a lasting relationship? These concerns make them afraid of being intimate.

CHAPTER - 21
THE 7 GOLDEN RULES FOR A HAPPY AND LASTING RELATIONSHIP

Find the Love in You!

You need to find and acknowledge love in yourself before you can share it with another. The sages and saints of all traditions have told us that love is within us, always and forever. The yogis of India say that there is a place in the center of your chest that is the gateway to an infinite ocean of inner love. Would you like to dive? All you need to do is sit quietly with your eyes closed. Then, bring up a memory of someone or something you love in your mind. Experience your feelings of love for that person, and let that sensation of love bring a warm smile to your lips. Just bask in the glow of that loving feeling for a few moments. Then smile at your body, appreciating it, feeling grateful for it. The Chinese sage invented this Inner Smile technique as a form of Chi Kung to bring health and wellness to the body. We are using it to feel wonderful and to saturate our being with a feeling of love. Bring that loving, smiling energy into the center of your chest. Imagine a small opening in the hollow of your chest that leads to that Infinite Love within. Sit in that space and just create a feeling of infinite love. Enjoy it. Dive into it. And above all, know that you can access and feel it at any time, simply by putting your attention and awareness there.

Pledge Your Allegiance to Love!

Now that you have discovered that eternal love is within you, you are free from being so needy and dependent on others for your happiness. You are already more attractive to be around.

Now, as far as how to improve your relationship, I think one main secret is that "commitment to love" that we've all so conveniently forgotten about. We have been fooled by romantic movies into thinking that love should be effortless and spontaneous, something we experience as an event. But love is a verb—it's something you do! And you can enjoy its incredible benefits if you make an effort to incorporate it into your life. You do it by making it a priority. Commit to love, and love will commit to you.

The Dance With the Beloved

Make an active show of being in love with your partner. Start saying "I love you" frequently throughout the day when you are around your partner. Give unexpected hugs and kisses. Do not stay there waiting for them to answer you. You may be doing all the "work" to begin with; It can be frustrating, but keep immersing yourself in that infinite love inside of you, okay?

Thank your partner every time he or she does something for you and show them an appreciation for the things they do in life and at home. If your relationship has been at a very low level, this can be arduous work, to begin with... but you are committed to this because you want that "feeling of love" back between you. I'm telling you to do this with your partner, but don't stop there— spread love through all your relationships: your children, your siblings, your parents or family, your friends, and co-workers. You deserve to improve all your relationships.

Symbols of Love

Now that love is your thing, support your relationship with reminder triggers and unconscious cues. The Chinese art of Feng Shui recommends that to improve your relationship, place images of happy couples in love in your bedroom (and remove any images of single people). You can also include those little figurines of couples hugging and kissing. I have been in the habit of buying one on every anniversary—and they are subconscious signals about the couple, togetherness, and intimacy.

What's in a Name?

Do you have a special name for your loved one? When you talk to your partner, if you haven't already, start including love labels, like "my love," "honey," "loved," and "lover." Some people use "baby," but do you want to be a mother to your partner? The same goes for calling your man "dad." Avoid mixing your metaphors in that way. Stick to the terms of equality.

Delete Your Clause

Throw away the "escape clause" you keep in the back of your mind. This is the thought that you can always leave this relationship if something better comes along, or you can leave if the other person doesn't fit your idea of what the relationship should be. Resolve right now to test this relationship against all odds. Never again bring the threat of leaving to an argument. We've been trained by too many TV dramas to think that if you argue, it has to turn into one big emotional explosion that leads to dramatic partings. It's so childish. Commit to resolve differences, return to a state of love, and lessen your need to prove yourself right and the other person wrong. Who cares! It's not worth it if it messes up the emotional tone of your union.

The Riches of Love

Invest in your relationship, and it will pay the biggest and best dividends of your life. Become a billionaire of love. Your search for the secrets of how to improve your relationship will be rewarded with an enriched relationship. End the pain and disappointment, and create the love you deserve in your life. Start by copying the strategies of the top 1% of couples who enjoy wonderful, loving relationships. Find out how to never have a fight again, save your marriage and grow deeper in love with each other.

CONCLUSION

We have looked at love and the pleasure it brings to the heart. Ameer said: "love doesn't hurt, only the person who doesn't know how to love hurts." Most of the fears that cause you to suffer can be controlled and resolved. Those fears that haunt your life daily were only learned and can be unlearned. You can control them whenever you want. It's just a matter of you preparing, deciding, and acting. Face your demons. Sometimes fear comes like a big mountain that you can't get over, you have no idea what to do but be brave, face it and you will realize that it wasn't as scary as you thought.

Habits of mind may seem ridiculous, but they are dangerous if not taken care of. Every mental habit drives your imagination, which can end up manifesting in reality. Let's look at a mental habit of imagining cheating on your partner. At first, it will be in your mind, but if you keep thinking the same thing repeatedly, you will end up running the imagination. Habits of mind instill fear that ultimately wreaks havoc on your life.

To the extent that fear is learned and can be unlearned, it is always good to take it easy while trying to overcome it. Rushing it can bring more disaster than before. It can cause you to land on the wrong remedies, which can worsen situations.

Not all remedies to overcome fear work for everyone. There are different types of fear; therefore, different solutions are used, just like when you are sick. If you have a bacterial infection, you cannot go to the pharmacy and buy anticancer drugs, this will not work. You must administer the appropriate medication so that the disease disappears.

As you overcome your fear, you don't need to resist your fears. Sometimes resisting them makes it worse. You can learn to surrender to your fear and come out stronger than before. When you come out stronger, you can push further and you will find that the fear is going away.

The problem arises when someone tries to cling to their fears and does not want to let go of them or does not want to surrender to them and use them as a springboard. If you can't let go of your fears or if you can't master a way to overcome them, you will never be free mentally, socially, and psychologically, where all this will harm your relationship and your life in general.

However, not everyone who faces their fears can overcome them at the expected or specific speed. There is nothing wrong when you take your time to overcome your fears. Everything has its time, and your fears have their time, and when it reaches you, you will be able to fight them.

Made in the USA
Las Vegas, NV
06 September 2022

JADE G.

54774037R00092